High Praise for Courage Goes to Work

"*Courage Goes to Work* helps solve the most perplexing management dilemma of all: how to inspire employees who are too comfortable and too afraid (or, as Bill says, comfeartable). Don't just read it . . . absorb it!
Lilicia P. Bailey, Chief People Officer, Manheim

"This book is truly awesome! Bill Treasurer has stolen courage from the gods and brought it to the workplace, where it is desperately needed. Everyone in a leadership role should put this book on their must-read list. After reading it, you may find the courage to buy a copy for your boss!"
Chip Bell, author of *Customer Loyalty Guaranteed*

"There are few business books that can truly be called transformative, and *Courage Goes to Work* is one of them. It offers tangible ideas for helping workers have more initiative, confidence, and backbone. If your employees could use more of those things, then this book is for you."
David Baruch, CIO, Hewitt Associates

"*Courage Goes to Work* is an excellent, well-written, and relevant book that captures the nuances of courage that will enable readers build courage—for themselves and for others. This is truly a thoughtful composition of the lessons learned on a figurative and literal high dive."
Chuck McManus, Vice President
(Fund of Hedge Funds Data Management), Morgan Stanley

"Courage is the first and most important component of success in business. Without it, there is nothing more than mediocrity and boredom. Bill Treasurer captures this awareness in his book and instructs us in making sure we're not overlooking that important aspect of fulfillment and success in our working life. Have the courage to leap, he says, even from dizzying heights. The water will embrace you and reward you. He knows—he's been there."
David Ryback, coauthor of *Psychology of Champions*

"Bill Treasurer is like a modern-day Wizard of Oz who helps to make us more courageous, not just at work, but in life. Instead of giving us medals to remind us not to be afraid, he offers buckets of specific tools that show us how to tap into our inner courage whenever and wherever we need it. This will be one of the most dog-eared books on my shelf. And it will hold a place of honor right next to his other gem, *Right Risk*."
Marilynn T. Mobley, Senior Vice President and Strategic Counsel,
Edelman & Associates

"You will not find a more clear voice on *courage* than Bill Treasurer's. Like Bill, I have worked for over a decade exploring courage in the high-risk realm of leader-follower relations with senior political figures and management teams. I do a good job of this at a foundational level. Bill's work is the graduate program. Let him guide you to the heights where your life and work become extraordinary—because you understand your fear and that of others and bring out the courage in each."
Ira Chaleff, author of *The Courageous Follower*

"Having spent over two decades in HR, I have seen a good number of books come and go. Only a handful really make you think, and *Courage Goes to Work* is one of them. It introduces an important new management practice: courage building. This powerful yet often-ignored concept can change the way people and organizations succeed. Put this book at the top of your management reading list—you'll be glad you did."

Keith Hicks, Vice President of Human Resources, Radiant Systems

"Even for people who are full of courage, instilling courage in others can be a daunting task. As someone who knows a thing or two about courage, I found this book is an invaluable tool every manager can and should use. The only thing worse than the quagmire of an office locked in comfort or fear is a manager too afraid to do something about it!"

Dustin Webster, seven-time world cliff-diving champion
and Executive Director, W.E. Rock Events, Inc.

"Bill Treasurer brings a true blend of wisdom, compassion, and personal experience to the understanding of courage and brings a practical approach to giving people the courage to stretch themselves and achieve great results. *Courage Goes to Work* raises people's standards so they can stop coasting along in the safety of 'good enough.'"

Conor Neill, CEO, Taxijet Spain, and Professor
of Managerial Communications, IESE Business School, Barcelona

"Whether you're facing a hundred-foot diving board or your board of directors, Bill's advice is practical, fun, and immediately applicable. His insightful and refreshing way of dealing with mental obstacles shows how fear, in both yourself and those around you, is nothing to be scared of."

Justin Roux, Senior Vice President, Luvata Group

"Courage is good for any industry. But when you work in the wicked world of drug law enforcement the stakes are even higher. In my field an absence of courage in an agent at any level, from those working the street to senior executives, can cost lives. It is great news that it turns out that courage can be taught—thanks to Bill Treasurer."

June W. Rodgers, retired special agent in charge, New England
Field Division, Drug Enforcement Administration

"*Courage Goes to Work* offers refreshing ideas about the most essential of all human qualities: courage. This is one of the rare business books that are relevant both personally and professionally. Read this book and go on the most important adventure of all—putting courage to work at your office, in your home, and in your life."

Bill Murray, Director, Outward Bound Professional,
North Carolina Outward Bound

"*Courage Goes to Work* is a must-read for anyone who needs to show up with strength at work every single day. This is an inspiring book about how we can all be a little more brave, authentic, and effective in our professional and personal lives. I was personally inspired by the message and will be recommending this book to everyone I know."

Brendon Burchard, author of *Life's Golden Ticket*

"Whenever I'm feeling a bit chicken, I need only pick up Bill's new book, *Courage Goes to Work*, and my own courage starts to rally. By the time I'm finished reading, I'm feeling like an eagle—ready to fly high and take on any challenge!"

BJ Gallagher, coauthor of *A Peacock in the Land of Penguins*

"Bill Treasurer is a peaceful warrior whose mission is to inspire others to take courageous action despite their fears. As a former combat fighter pilot, I am intimately familiar with what courage can do for the success of individuals and teams who work in high-pressure environments. Bill's book is a compelling read and is packed full of thought-provoking, real-world anecdotes and simple yet powerful action steps to build courage at work. It's one of a kind."

Waldo Waldman, decorated fighter pilot and professional speaker

"What I love about *Courage Goes to Work* is its pragmatism. Courage is often seen as something inborn that only people like skydivers or serial entrepreneurs have. Bill Treasurer shows us that courage is a learned behavior that managers can teach through daily practice."

Jonathon Flaum, Director, WriteMind Institute for
Corporate Contemplation; author of *How the Paper Fish Learned to Swim* and
How the Red Wolf Found Its Howl; and coauthor of *The 100-Mile Walk*

"Finally, a practical and inspiring book about the virtue that is perhaps most needed yet most lacking in the world today: courage. If you ever wish that you could overcome your apprehensions and fears so that you could more fully reach your potential and dreams, a good place to start is to read this book."

Charles C. Manz, author of *The Power of Failure* and
The Leadership Wisdom of Jesus, and coauthor of
The Virtuous Organization and *Nice Guys Can Get the Corner Office*

"In *Courage Goes to Work* Bill Treasurer takes a mysterious and complex subject that touches everyone and breaks it into bite-size, manageable chunks. Looking at the small pieces enables you to take care of the critical task we all face—moving toward what we have feared and avoided in the past. Buy this book today and take action tomorrow!"

Stewart Levine, Resolutionary, author of *Getting to Resolution*
and *The Book of Agreement*, and coauthor of *Collaboration 2.0*

"How do you motivate people who are too comfortable or too afraid? This is a common question from managers and supervisors. In *Courage Goes to Work* Bill Treasurer provides practical answers to this question. He points out that to instill courage is to encourage and wants you, as a manager, to become a chief encourager. Drawing on his experience as a seasoned business consultant and stunt diver, he will show you how. This book should be on every manager's bookshelf."

> Cindy Ventrice, author of *Make Their Day!*

"To live and work in a world of accelerated change requires individual courage. Bill Treasurer captures the essence of courage in his newest book, *Courage Goes to Work*. He takes an attribute that others might think is ethereal and makes it concrete. He illustrates how anyone can access their courage and how others can create an environment where courageous behavior can flourish. With an abundance of courage, individual and organizational greatness can be achieved!"

> Leslie Yerkes, President, Catalyst Consulting Group, Inc.,
> and author of *Fun Works*

"*Courage Goes to Work* is an insightful call to summoning courage in self and courage in others. This is a very insightful guide, blending Treasurer's expertise in areas of risk and courage and harnessing their impact for increased results, performance, and effectiveness."

> Harry E. Chambers, author of *My Way or the Highway*

"Bill Treasurer has a deep understanding of courage, and after reading *Courage Goes to Work*, so will you."

> Noah Blumenthal, President, Leading Principles, Inc.,
> and author of *You're Addicted to You*

"Most of us take our minds to work but leave courage at the door. In this compelling book, Bill Treasurer provides three nourishing lunch buckets to take to work everyday, try courage, trust courage, and tell courage. In doing so, you'll have all you need to be a better person and a better leader."

> Dick Axelrod, author of *Terms of Engagement*

"If ever there were a book that business and nonprofit executives need to read, this is it. Courage is every bit as important to an organization as leadership, innovation, and focus are, and this little gem is chock-full of powerful ideas that could transform your people and your workplace. Prepare to be en-couraged in unexpected ways!"

> Sam Pettway, Founding Director, BoardWalk Consulting

COURAGE GOES TO WORK

**How to Build
Backbones,
Boost Performance,
and Get Results**

BILL TREASURER

BK

Berrett–Koehler Publishers, Inc.
San Francisco
a BK Business book

Berrett-Koehler Publishers, Inc.
235 Montgomery Street, Suite 650
San Francisco, CA 94104-2916
Tel: (415) 288-0260   Fax: (415) 362-2512   www.bkconnection.com

Ordering Information

Quantity sales. Special discounts are available on quantity purchases by corporations, associations, and others. For details, contact the "Special Sales Department" at the Berrett-Koehler address above.

Individual sales. Berrett-Koehler publications are available through most bookstores. They can also be ordered directly from Berrett-Koehler: Tel: (800) 929-2929; Fax: (802) 864-7626; www.bkconnection.com

Orders for college textbook/course adoption use. Please contact Berrett-Koehler: Tel: (800) 929-2929; Fax: (802) 864-7626.

Orders by U.S. trade bookstores and wholesalers. Please contact Ingram Publisher Services, Tel: (800) 509-4887; Fax: (800) 838-1149; E-mail: customer.service@ingrampublisherservices.com; or visit www.ingrampublisherservices.com/Ordering for details about electronic ordering.

Berrett-Koehler and the BK logo are registered trademarks of Berrett-Koehler Publishers, Inc.

Printed in the United States of America

Berrett-Koehler books are printed on long-lasting acid-free paper. When it is available, we choose paper that has been manufactured by environmentally responsible processes. These may include using trees grown in sustainable forests, incorporating recycled paper, minimizing chlorine in bleaching, or recycling the energy produced at the paper mill.

Library of Congress Cataloging-in-Publication Data

Treasurer, Bill, 1962-

Courage goes to work : how to build backbones, boost performance, and get results / Bill Treasurer.

    p. cm.

Includes index.

ISBN 978-1-57675-501-3 (hbk. : alk. paper)

    1. Management—Psychological aspects. 2. Personnel management—Psychological aspects. 3. Employees—Attitudes. 4. Courage. 5. Organizational change—Management. I. Title.

HD31.T6826 2008

658.3´14—dc22   2008025608

First Edition

12 11 10 09 08   10 9 8 7 6 5 4 3 2 1

Text design by Detta Penna
Copyediting by Elissa Rabellino
Proofreading by Susan Padgett
Index by Joan Dickey

Contents

*Dedicated to Alex, Bina, and Ian,
my three heartbeats.
In all you do, Be Courageous.*

*And to Olivia Grace, our cherub in heaven.
You are with us always.*

Foreword

by Sara Blakely, founder of SPANX

"What on earth am I doing?!"

The mind tries to make sense at the strangest times. The irony was, I wasn't on earth . . . I was ten thousand feet in the air climbing up the side of a hot air balloon on a dangling rope ladder. (Yes, the girl who is afraid of heights and sometimes cries during airplane takeoffs.)

What led me to that moment? Well, there's a short answer and a longer one. The short answer is that I was competing for $1 million as a reality show contestant on Sir Richard Branson's television show, *The Rebel Billionaire*. The long answer is that my whole life had been preparing me for a moment like this.

The value of courage was taught to me at an early age. Lessons about courage, in my household, were every bit as important as lessons about history or arithmetic. At the dinner table, my dad would ask my brother and me, "So, kids, what did you *fail* at this week?" If we didn't have a good answer, he'd be disappointed. If we had failed—for example, "Dad, I tried out for this and I was horrible"—he would congratulat us and give us a big high five! Knowing that my parents supported and *expected* me to take risks took the fear out of failing.

One of my earliest memories of doing something courageous was in the sixth grade, when I had to transfer to a new school. I was afraid of change. I had been with the same

group of friends since I was five, and starting over was terrifying. Knowing that my "crazy" dad encouraged us to fail, I
did the most courageous thing I could think of: I ran for class
president…after attending the school for only one week!
When I told my mom about my plan to run for president, she
gently said, "But sweetie, you might not win." She was right.
In fact, I was almost guaranteed to lose. Through that experience, so many wonderful things happened. Among them,
I immediately earned the respect of the new students and
made fast friends. After a few months, no one remembered
that I had lost the run for president; they just remembered
me. I started to "get it."

Now don't get me wrong—although I consider myself a courageous person, I am scared of almost everything.
Through the years, I have developed a mantra: "Sara, if you
weren't afraid, would you do it?" If the answer is yes, I take
a deep breath and do it! I made a pact with myself long ago
that I would never let fear get in the way of moving my life
forward. Courage, not the absence of fear, is just doing it anyway.

All this doesn't mean that I am fearless or reckless. It just
means that if the road in front of me looks scary, I take fear
along for the ride—but I keep on moving, *with* the fear. In every situation where I was ever courageous, you could just as
easily substitute the word *afraid* for *courageous*. I was afraid,
for example, when I started SPANX with $5,000 in savings. I
was afraid when I knocked on the doors of textile mills beg-
ging them to manufacture my prototype for a new footless
pantyhose (for which I had written and earned a patent). I
was afraid when I stood in front of the hot TV cameras on the
QVC network for the first time. I was afraid when I traveled to

Dallas with my lucky red backpack to meet the buyer at Neiman Marcus to interest her in selling SPANX products. I was afraid the first time I was a guest on *The Oprah Winfrey Show*. I was afraid when I did the same thing at Saks, Nordstrom, and Bloomingdale's. I was afraid when I called on Target and suggested that SPANX create a new product line for them called ASSETS. And I was afraid as I inched my way up a flimsy rope ladder on the side of a billowy hot air balloon.

Why do these things? Because courage has never let me down. Courage has brought me great friends, kept life fabulously interesting, and earned me a healthy income. The way I look at it, you are the writer, director, and producer of your own life. I don't want my movie to be boring. Courage ensures that it won't.

Courage has been so important to my life that I've made instilling courage in others a top priority at SPANX. First, I try to be a courageous role model. People respond with courage of their own when they see me take chances and step up to challenges. Second, when people make mistakes, especially mistakes made by taking risks to move the company forward, I'm never disappointed. Instead, I go up to them and give them a big high five! The third way I instill courage at SPANX is to introduce SPANX's employees to new and original ideas, particularly if those ideas advance SPANX's mission of promoting confidence in women. Bill Treasurer's ideas about courage and risk taking resonated so strongly with the SPANX team that we ended up working with Bill and the Giant Leap team on three separate occasions. By our encouraging people to constantly try new and challenging things, and by our associating with companies that reinforce our values, the $5,000 investment that started SPANX from the back of my apartment grew into a $200 million business. Yep, courage is good business.

How can you fill people with enough confidence that they'll set aside their fears and do extraordinary things? What can you do to put courage to work for you and the people you lead? Reading *Courage Goes to Work* is a great start. To be successful in business, you need great mentors—people who've "been there" and can help you to "go there." Bill's unique insights about courage come from unusual and hard-earned experiences, inside and outside of work. By drawing on his own courageous experiences, as well as on the work he's done with clients like SPANX, Bill has developed a practical way of understanding, categorizing, and inspiring courageous behavior.

I'm a big reader of books about human performance. Too many of them, though, are both unrealistic and unfulfilling. They tell you obvious things, like "Don't be afraid!" or "Tell yourself you're brave, and you will be!" What makes *Courage Goes to Work* so appealing is that it respects your intelligence by acknowledging that fear and comfort are business (and behavioral) realities. It offers specific suggestions for working *with* those realities instead of brushing them aside as though they don't matter. For managers, because they deal with the negative consequences of workers' fear and comfort on a daily basis, this book is particularly useful. By providing managers with specific advice for building people's courage, the book strengthens the backbones of managers and workers alike. The result is what every business strives for: higher confidence, higher morale, and higher aim.

To be sure, courage can come with payoffs. But don't be surprised if those payoffs come in the form of even greater and scarier challenges. My reward for summiting Richard

Branson's hot air balloon, which after forty-five terrifying minutes I eventually did, was the opportunity to travel to Africa. The catch? I had to dive into the outstretched arms of a fellow contestant—after leaping off a 380-foot cliff. As the saying goes, "Just another day at the office!"

Oh, but did I mention that I was runner-up and Richard Branson surprised me with his personal paycheck of $750,000? I used the money to launch the Sara Blakely Foundation to help women and, among other things, sent 278 women to college in South Africa. So this is how transformative it can be when courage goes to work. One courageous moment on your part just might end up having a far greater impact than you could ever have imagined.

Too Much Comfort, Too Much Fear

Courage is the thing. All goes if courage goes.

Joseph Addison

We have not journeyed across the centuries, across the oceans, across the mountains, across the prairies, because we are made of sugar candy.

Winston Churchill

"Management sucks. And I'm a manager, so I guess I suck too. Or the people I'm managing suck. Either way, this ain't fun and I want out."

It was discouraging to see that Brian's situation had deteriorated to this point. Only two years earlier, Brian had been fast-tracked into a front-line manager position. His upbeat attitude and make-it-happen work ethic had caught the attention of the company executives, who decided that he'd make a fine addition to their ranks. Yet here he was, ready to jump ship. And he hated himself for it.

"For the first time in my life, I feel like a failure. I couldn't wait to be made a manager. But now I'm convinced that I'm not cut out for it. I think the only reason I haven't quit already is because I'm too ashamed, or too competitive, to admit defeat. I hate being a manager."

I had been coaching Brian for a few months as part of a multiyear leadership program my company had developed for Brian's employer. The program had been developed for the company's high-potential leaders, and Brian had been handpicked by his boss to participate. Brian was highly regarded by the senior executives, so it was a bit surprising for me to hear that things had gotten so bad for him. Somehow this "hi-po" manager had been able to conceal his true feelings about the job from his boss and coworkers.

"It surprises me that you don't think you're cut out to be a manager, Brian. Is it the work? The pressure? What?" I asked.

"The pressure I can deal with. I was a college athlete and I kind of like pressure. It makes things seem more important and urgent, which gets me going. And the tactical part of the work, for the most part, isn't hard. You make a plan; you break it down into a set of goals, milestones, and delivery dates; you keep it all organized on a spreadsheet; and then you work the plan."

"So what's the crux of it, buddy?" I asked. "From what you just told me, you don't find management all that hard. What I didn't hear about was the stuff you hate about managing. What about that?"

Like lava inching its way up through the earth, the frustrations that had gotten Brian to this point began bubbling to the surface. "To me, the hard part about managing, the stuff I *hate*, is all the people stuff. I hate the fact that no one shows the initiative to take on work outside their own scope. I hate the small way people think, and how the only thing they seem to care about is the itty-bitty task right in front of them. I hate having to continuously remind people about impending deadlines and that no one works with the same urgency or intensity as I do. I hate having to force people to accept changes that the company requires us to make and that are mostly in everyone's best interests. I hate all the psychoanalyzing that goes into figuring out how to get people to trust me. I also hate not being able to trust that people won't screw up and make me look bad when I assign important tasks to them. I hate having to confront people about their performance, especially when they think they're performing way better than they really are. I hate having to pry the truth out of people so that I know about problems before it's too late to solve them. And I especially hate all the crybaby excuses, finger-pointing, and shitty attitudes that get in the way of doing actual work."

The little venting moment helped Brian to purge all the surface stuff so that he could get closer to the core of the issue. After a moment his eyes got smaller, as if he'd found a shiny golden nugget while prospecting at the center of hell. He continued, "When it comes right down to it, I hate that people are either too comfortable doing things the way they've always done them or too afraid to do things differently."

Mixing Comfort and Fear

Over the years, I've coached a lot of people like Brian. Talented workers who get promoted because of their strong leadership potential, but who quickly grow frustrated with managing people who are slow to change, slow to trust, and slow getting things done. Brian's golden nugget insight is spot-on: The problem has to do with comfort and fear. Workers who are too comfortable don't exert themselves any more than they have to. They become satisfied meeting a minimum standard of performance, equating "just enough" with good enough. Like a sofa loaded down with overstuffed relatives after a holiday dinner, teams with workers who are too comfortable become lethargic and heavy with the weight of mediocrity. At the same time, workers who are too fearful play it too safe. Fearful workers set *safe* goals, say *safe* things, and make *safe* choices. Because fearful workers spend far too much energy preserving what is instead of pursuing what could be, their preoccupation with safety ultimately becomes dangerous for the business.

Comfort and fear in smaller doses can be good things. Striving to gain comfort with new skills, for example, is a worthwhile goal. At the same time, fear helps workers to focus on preventing and mitigating risks by keeping them vigilant about small issues that could grow into big problems. But in higher doses, and especially when mixed together, comfort and fear become toxic, creating a situation where workers become what I call "com*fear*table."

Com*fear*table workers are those who grow comfortable working in a perpetual state of fear, which only serves to magnify the ill effects of both concepts. Com*fear*table workers develop a high tolerance for misery, often staying in jobs they don't find gratifying or, worse yet, secretly despise. Some com*fear*table workers are like impassive zombies, sleepwalking through their jobs with no sense of urgency or commitment. Others include excuse makers, people who choose apathy over action by cooking up all sorts of reasons why they can't do something instead of just doing it. Com*feart*-

able workers also include people who dump problems in your lap but offer no solutions for solving them. For these workers, going the extra mile just takes too much effort. Instead, com*fear*table workers give their deepest fidelity to safety and sameness, even if those things come at the expense of progress. When fused together, comfort and fear adhere to the same law: *Stay safe at all costs!* No initiative. No risk taking. No candor. No making waves. No more than what is asked. No innovating or extending or leading. And no support for those who do.

This book is for all the managers like Brian out there. Maybe you're one of them. If you've grown frustrated trying to get workers to stretch beyond their comfort zones, if you're at your wits' end trying to get workers to step up to their potential, or if you're tired of having to treat adults like frightened children, this book is for you.

Activating Com*fear*table Workers

As a manager, you may be tempted to adopt a scorched-earth campaign and just fire all the com*fear*table workers. But a wholesale firing of such workers would do more harm than good. Com*fear*table workers are so prevalent in the workplace that such a strategy would be the managerial equivalent of carpet bombing, potentially eviscerating the organization. A more constructive and practical approach would be to help workers face and overcome their com*fear*table ways. The reality is, managing workers who are overly comfortable or fearful is the essence of management. At the core, management is all about transforming and inspiring com*fear*table workers. All the other stuff—the planning, goal setting,

> »
> Your success as a manager will be determined by how well you manage workers who are too comfortable, too afraid, or too much of both.
> »

organizing, and delivering—is just the minimum requirement for entry into the management ranks. The hard stuff, the stuff that will determine your success and longevity as a manager, pertains to how you manage the funky behavioral effects of workers who are too comfortable, too afraid, or too much of both. The bottom line is this: Your success and happiness as a manager depend on how you manage com*fear*table workers.

My guess is that your company put you in a management position because it thinks you've got a lot of promise as an executive. It thinks that in some small way you'll help move the company forward by advancing the goals you've been tasked with. To do that, you'll need to find new and better ways to get a greater return on your workers' passion, engagement, and initiative. You'll need to inspire greater commitment to company changes. You'll need to learn how to make people less afraid of stepping up to challenges, more willing to trust you and the company, and more apt to speak up candidly and assertively. The good news is, this book is designed to do all those things by promoting the antidote to com*fear*table behavior: courage.

Courage is, most often, a behavioral response to a challenge. It is something that has to be *activated* within us. Courage is called forth by challenge, opportunity, and hardship. It is also called forth by managers, mentors, and coaches who hold us accountable to our own potential by compelling us to achieve higher standards. As a manager, you have a responsibility, indeed an obligation, to activate the courage of those around you. Courage activation is your job.

Three Buckets of Courage

As mentioned, courage involves behavior. Like all behaviors, courage can be developed, encouraged, and reinforced. While a lot of writers have focused on the realms in which courage is applied (for example, moral courage, military courage, and political courage), I think it is more useful to understand the common ways that people behave when being courageous, regardless of which realm they're operating in. While the realms themselves may have sharp differences, the *ways* people behave when being courageous within those realms are surprisingly similar.

In my work as a courage-building consultant, I have discovered that there are three ways of behaving when your courage is activated. When you become familiar with the three distinct types of courageous behavior, you gain a deeper understanding of how to tap into, and strengthen, your own courage and the courage of those around you. I call these three different forms of courage the Three Buckets of Courage.

> *TRY* **Courage:** When managers talk about wanting workers to "step up to the plate," it is *TRY* Courage that they are referring to. *TRY* Courage is the courage of initiative and action. You often see *TRY* Courage when people make "first attempts"—for example, whenever you see someone attempt new, skill-stretching, or pioneering tasks. Someone who volunteers to lead a tough or risky project is demonstrating *TRY* Courage.

> *TRUST* **Courage:** *TRUST* Courage is the courage that it takes to relinquish control and rely on others. When managers talk of wanting employees to embrace

company changes more willingly or to follow directives more enthusiastically, it is more *TRUST* Courage that they want employees to have. When *TRUST* Courage is present, people give each other the benefit of the doubt, instead of questioning the motives and intentions of those around them. *TRUST* Courage isn't about taking charge (as with *TRY* Courage), but about following the charge of others.

TELL **Courage:** *TELL* Courage is the courage of "voice," and involves speaking with candor and conviction, especially when the opinions expressed run counter to the group's. To preserve their safety, workers often agree too much and speak out too little. When *TELL* Courage is activated, it causes workers to assert themselves more willingly and confidently. You see *TELL* Courage at work when employees tactfully but truthfully provide tough feedback . . . even to you, their manager. You also see it when workers raise their hands and ask for help, or when they tell you about mistakes they've made before you ask.

The main benefit of using the Three Buckets of Courage as a framework for understanding and categorizing courageous behavior is that it helps make courage, as a concept, more graspable. Courage is a large and vague concept. Using the *TRY, TRUST, TELL* framework helps bring it down to size. Parsing courage into three behavioral buckets allows us to discriminate the different ways we have been courageous in the past and are capable of being in the future. Think, for example, of the scariest or most uncomfortable moments in your career thus far. Weren't you *try*ing something new, *trust*ing someone else's lead, and/or *tell*ing the truth about a conviction you were upholding? Now think about the single biggest career goal you have in front of you right now. To achieve your goal, won't it involve exercising more *TRY*, *TRUST*, or *TELL* Courage (or some combination of all three)? Now think about your com*fear*table workers. Wouldn't having more *TRY*, *TRUST*, and *TELL* Courage help them to move past the debilitating effects of comfort and fear?

The Three Buckets of Courage are explained in greater detail in part 2 of the book. For now, it is enough to know that the best way to get workers to try new things, trust you more fully, and tell you what they're really thinking is to build up their courage. Consider, for example, what would happen if all your com*fear*table workers started putting their courage buckets to work. With more *TRY* Courage, wouldn't workers take on more skill-stretching projects? With more *TRUST* Courage, wouldn't they embrace company changes with more enthusiasm and less resistance? If people used more *TELL* Courage, wouldn't they speak up more frequently and truthfully? And by using all three types of courage, wouldn't workers be less risk averse, less self-conscious, and less apathetic? Wouldn't having more courage also result in less brown-nosing, ass covering, and shitty attitudes? Most important, with more *TRY*, *TRUST*, and *TELL* Courage, wouldn't workers stop being so comfortably afraid?

» **This book is about the actions that you and your workers can take to be more courageous, and what you can do to foster more courageous behavior at work.**

»

When Courage Goes to Work

The payoff for helping your workers to become more coura-geous, the ultimate aim of this book, is that it makes your job easier and more rewarding. So what does it look like when courage goes to work? You see courage working when people trust your decisions instead of silently resisting your every move. Courage is working when employees raise the red flag on projects that are going south instead of hiding issues until they fester into full-blown catastrophes. Courage is working when employees come to you with remedies to problems they are facing, instead of dumping problems in your lap. You see courage working when people are candid and engaged dur-ing status meetings, instead of politely nodding their heads "yes" every time you talk. You see courage working whenever you see people trying things outside their skill sets, or delib-erately seeking out leadership opportunities, or offering ideas for expanding the team's reach. When courage goes to work, you see engagement, and passion, and motivation, and com-mitment. You also see shaking knees and hear shaky voices. Stepping into one's courage, for most workers, is a scary and uncomfortable thing. Being courageous requires encourage-ment—from the company, from each other, and from you.

Part of your job is to be a manager. But an equally im-portant part of your job is to be an encourager—to put cour-age inside people. When you fill up people's buckets with courage—when you encourage them—they place less of a premium on comfort and begin to purposely seek out skill-stretching challenges. With full buckets of courage, they come to value the energy that fear provides as a necessary fuel for doing uncomfortable things. When people are full of courage, they're much more likely to *TRY* new things, *TRUST* you more fully, and *TELL* the truth more candidly. As I explain in chapter 6, the more courage you fill people with, the less com*fear*table workers will be.

The Consequences of Courage

As one of the world's only courage-building consultants, I am an unabashed and vocal advocate for bringing more courage to the workplace. But I readily admit that behaving courageously often comes with unintended consequences. While it is true that people can find their courage when facing challenging and dangerous situations, it is equally true that behaving courageously can bring new challenges and dangers of its own. Workers can get fired for making mistakes, blindly following errant directives, or disagreeing too vocally, regardless of how sincere their intentions for doing so are. But those rare instances shouldn't overshadow the fact that, on balance, people who act courageously at work are more successful than those who don't.

The purpose of this book isn't to cause you to fearlessly swagger into your boss's office, kick your boots up on her desk, and start rattling off all the reasons why she and the company need to change. Courage for courage's sake is at best gratuitous. To be productive and beneficial, courage needs direction and discipline. This book is about providing you with the tips, tools, and techniques that will help you to find the courage that's inside you and apply it in ways that strengthen your career.

The Groundwork

Before diving in, it might help you to know how the book is organized. Part 1, consisting of the first five chapters, reinforces the importance and value of putting courage to work. Chapter 1 introduces a model that will help you to build a foundation that encourages courageous behavior. In chapter 2, you'll learn how Jumping First (that is, being a good role model of courageous behavior) strengthens the courage of those around you. Chapter 3 shows you how to construct safety nets in order to support people as they take on more challenging things. Chapter 4 discusses ways to harness fear as a useful, productive, and even energizing managerial tool. Chapter 5 provides tips for helping workers to modulate between comfort and discomfort.

Part 2 of the book dimensionalizes the Three Buckets of Courage concept. Chapter 6 offers ideas for putting the buckets concept to work. Distinctions are also made between two types of management dispositions: *Fillers* and *Spillers*. Chapters 7, 8, and 9 illustrate, through real-life stories and client examples, the Three Buckets of Courage. Chapter 7 covers *TRY* Courage, chapter 8 reviews *TRUST* Courage, and chapter 9 discusses *TELL* Courage.

Part 3, comprising chapters 10 and 11, starts by providing you with two contrasting views of the same workplace—one directed by fear, the other infused with courage—so that you can make an informed choice about the management approach you will use going forward. The contrasting views, as well as other rationales for putting courage to work, are presented in chapter 10. Finally, chapter 11 looks at courage in broader terms, so that you can take courage home with you after a long day at the office.

All the stories you'll read about in the book involve real people facing real challenges. Some people met their challenges with courage; others did not. In most instances I was at liberty to share both the names of the people in the stories and the names of the companies they work for. In some instances, however, either to preserve client confidences or to prevent people from embarrassment, I have changed their names. As a general rule, when both their first and last names are included in the story, it is their actual name. When only their first name is referred to, the name is fictitious.

The Bottom Line on the Top Virtue

Aristotle called courage the first virtue because it makes all the other virtues possible. If that is true, then courage is also the first virtue of business. Courage, after all, is the lifeblood of leadership, entrepreneurialism, and innovation. In fact, courage is so critical to these things that they can't exist without it.

While courage may be the premier business virtue, in many workplaces it is desperately lacking. Workers are either too comfortable to change or too afraid to try new things. Or, as explained in this introduction, they are both comfortable and fearful at the same time. When workers' actions are directed by comfort and fear, underperformance will always be the result. As a manager, you need to be keenly aware of the dangers that comfort and fear present, and equipped with strategies for mitigating them.

In the coming pages, you will be provided with strategies and tips for influencing workers to be more courageous. Doing so will help them gain the necessary confidence to take on

more difficult projects, assume leadership roles more readily, embrace company changes with more enthusiasm, and
extend themselves in ways that will benefit their careers and
your team. The bottom line is this: Putting courage to work
will cause your workers to stop being so com*fear*table, and
help you to be a better, more effective, and happier manager.

»   «

The Five Promises of Workforce Courage

There are five premises upon which this book was written.
But they are more than premises; they are promises. I call
them the five promises of workforce courage, and this book
aims to champion and uphold them. They are as follows:

1. **Everyone** has the capacity to be courageous.

2. **Employees perform better** when they are
   working courageously.

3. **Courage** is a learnable and teachable skill.

4. **The key** to putting courage to work is the
   regimen of things you regularly do before
   challenging situations present themselves.

5. **The entire workforce** benefits when
   everyone is showing up to work with more
   courage.

»   «

Part I

Setting a Foundation for Courage

People won't start being courageous just because you tell them to. You've got to create an environment that encourages them to extend themselves and take chances. In this section, you'll be introduced to four actions you need to take before expecting people to be more courageous. These four actions, introduced briefly at the end of chapter 1, constitute the Courage Foundation Model, and they follow a specific order.

The first action deals with role modeling, or what I call *Jumping First*. Why on earth would you expect people to be courageous if you yourself are wimpy? Your own courageous actions will have the biggest impact on people's willingness to be courageous.

The second action deals with creating safety. People won't take chances unless they have at least some degree of support from you. Getting people to take big leaps requires putting some safety nets in place to soften their landing.

Action number three deals with putting fear to work. Few things are as potent as fear in causing people to be risk averse. But fear has energy. Properly harnessed, fear's energy can be used to help people accomplish and overcome the very thing that may be inspiring their fear. The third action of the Courage Foundation Model is about harnessing fear.

The final action in the model deals with adjusting the degree of comfort and discomfort that workers experience. The idea is to slowly but persistently stretch workers' capacity to deal with uncomfortable situations by assigning them incrementally greater challenges. Doing so causes them to exert more courage in order to meet the challenging assignments.

Chapter 1

Look Before You Leap

The most dangerous strategy is to jump into a chasm in two leaps.

Benjamin Disraeli

Dustin Webster was scared; that much was clear. It was un-usual to see him this way. Dustin is the kind of employee that a supervisor dreams of. A real go-getter, Dustin always got to work on time (often early), undeterred by the Seattle traffic and unfazed by Seattle's soggy mariner weather. With Dustin, such things never prompted grousing or pessimism. He had more important things on his mind, like pitching in, helping out, and getting the job done. So seeing Dustin scared, really *scared*, was way out of pattern.

Looking back on it now, I'm sure Dustin's fear had something to do with the nature of the task. For Dustin, this was a pioneering endeavor. While he had plenty of skills to draw upon, and he had confronted plenty of other work challenges, this assignment went well beyond Dustin's comfort zone and into foreign terrain.

Firsts often provoke fear. I'm sure that Dustin had felt the same fearful feelings on his first day of school, or the first time he drove a car, or the first time he kissed a girl. These feelings were also at work the first time he led one of our team meetings, or the time I tapped him to be in charge when I got called out of town to temporarily lead another project.

Because I was Dustin's manager, my job was to help him temper his fear so that he could focus on the task at hand. I had to keep his potential at the forefront of my thinking. In a real way, I had to believe in Dustin's potential more than he believed in it himself. While his own doubt was inevitable, I would have to keep mine at bay lest we double the doubt, and in so doing, double the chances of Dustin failing. And failure, in this case, could have catastrophic consequences.

Yes, Dustin was scared, and he had a right to be. In a moment, he would attempt a triple twisting back double somersault after leaping backward from a tiny platform more than one hundred feet above the surface of a small pool. He'd be traveling at a velocity of over fifty miles per hour, a breakneck speed that could quite literally break his neck. Dustin and I were members of the U.S. High Diving Team.

Surprisingly, the things Dustin did to prepare for his big leap, and the things I did to coach him through it, were little different from the things workers and managers need to do to help them stop being com*fear*table. The big leap that Dustin was facing was a huge feat, but it wasn't entirely outside the realm of his experience. The dive was just the next logical step in the progression of his skills and capabilities, and the culmi-

nation of *lead-ups*—less complex dives from lower heights—
that he had taken over time. Plus, we had spent weeks pre-
paring for this moment, building his confidence in a way that,
metaphorically, lowered his high dive. Dustin first practiced
doing takeoffs from the pool deck. Then we had him adjust
the movable high-dive platform (called a *perch*) to ten feet
above the water. Once he got comfortable with his takeoff
from that height, we had him move it up twenty more feet.
The process involved purposely moving from comfort to discomfort and back again. Once he got comfortable with one
height, we'd stretch the height to a point of discomfort until
the new height became comfortable, too. Each time Dustin
got comfortable again, it was time for him to move up . . . we
both knew the dangers of his becoming too comfortable!

My job in all of this was to be Dustin's chief encourager—literally, to help put courage in him. That meant I had to
keep both of us focused on what Dustin had already done and
what he was capable of doing. It would have done no good for
me to stand on the pool deck yelling up to him about all the
things he *shouldn't* do. Yelling "Don't do this!" and "Don't do
that!" would have kept him looking in the wrong direction.
Instead, my coaching centered on the things he *should* do to
make the dive happen.

Keep in mind that as the captain of the team, I had a
vested interest in Dustin's succeeding. This was the U.S. High
Diving Team's first year at the Seattle amusement park. If
Dustin landed the dive, he would be one of a handful of people
in the world to have done so, a distinction that would impress
our audiences—and our amusement park client. It would look
very good for me if our client would re-sign our multimillion-
dollar contract at the end of the season, and Dustin's big dive

could go a long way toward making that happen. Dustin's win would be my win, too. Indeed, the team's win.

Despite all the preparation and encouragement, Dustin was still scared. Even though down deep he knew he was ready, doing such a complicated dive from this height wasn't going to come easy. The funny thing is, after I had cheered him on from the sidelines with little success, getting Dustin to launch the dive into the air took only a simple poolside coaxing technique, a method you'll probably remember from the first time you were cajoled off the high diving board at your local pool. Looking up at Dustin, I formed a bullhorn with my hands and yelled, "Okay, Dustin, it's time. Put your arms out to the sides. On the count of three, you're going to get this dive off the platform. All you have to do is get the dive in the air and let it do the work. The dive wants to dive. Ready? One . . . two . . . three . . . JUMP!"

And with that, Dustin leaped into the air, performing a gorgeous triple twisting back double somersault!

Workplace High Dives

Dustin Webster would go on to become a seven-time world cliff diving champion, even beating the Mexicans in Acapulco on their home cliffs. At first glance, his experience learning a triple twisting back double off a hundred-foot high-dive ladder may seem remote from your work environment. The reality, though, is that throughout their careers, workers are asked to perform "high dives" that carry both upside and downside consequences. Asking a worker to move into a new role in a new division is a high dive. Putting a worker in charge of a key customer account is a high dive. Having a worker give a presentation to your boss's management team is a high dive. Putting a worker in charge of your team while you go on maternity leave is a high dive. Informing a worker that she is one of three people being considered as your successor is a high dive. One person's triple twisting back double somersault is another's must-win sale, or do-or-die project, or failure-is-not-an-option strategic initiative. High dives come in many forms, including skill-stretching jobs, big consequential assignments, and sweeping organizational changes. In each case, when employees face such challenges confidently and courageously, a positive outcome is more likely than if they don't. In each case, a positive outcome is mutually beneficial to them, to you, and to the company. And in each case, the best way to get them to do their high dive is to get them to move beyond comfort and fear.

Courageously Fearful

As a former member of the U.S. High Diving Team, I learned firsthand the benefits of moving past my com*fear*table tendencies. Every day for seven years I would climb to the top of a hundred-foot high-dive ladder (the equivalent of a ten-story building) and stand atop a one-foot-by-one-foot perch. Then, after a quick prayer, I would leap into the air like an eagle taking flight. Except eagles soar upward. I never did. I would always go down, careening at speeds of over fifty miles per hour into a pool that was only ten feet deep. Fifteen hundred high dives, all done with no parachute, no bungee, and no safety gear. Just me, a thin coat of sunscreen, and a Speedo.

The fact that I was a high diver doesn't qualify me to write about courage. The fact that I was a high diver who is *afraid of heights* does. Becoming a high diver was a culmination of a series of things I did to engage with, learn from, and ultimately dominate my fear of heights. Many of the lessons I learned from this experience are chronicled in my first book, *Right Risk: 10 Powerful Principles for Taking Giant Leaps with Your Life* (Berrett-Koehler Publishers, 2003). The book's front cover has a picture of me diving while on fire. No kidding.

The experience and personal benefits I gained from dominating my fears taught me the supreme value of courage. While I am hardly the patron saint of courageous acts, I cherish courage above all other virtues. I have the Gaelic word for courage, *misneach*, prominently tattooed on my upper back . . . it helps remind me of my feisty Celtic heritage. Also, I am the only person in North Carolina to have a courage license. More specifically, my personalized North Carolina license plate is the word *COURAGE* (wave if you pass me!). Finally, three years ago, I forced a little courage on my family, moving us away from most of my clients in Atlanta, Georgia, and up to the Blue Ridge Mountains of Asheville, North Carolina. Why? So that we could all live more sanely . . . and pry ourselves loose from Atlanta's traffic lunacy.

I'm so convinced of the importance of courage to business success that in 2002, after working as a change-management consultant for over a decade, I founded Giant Leap Consulting, a courage-building company. Our mission, like the aim of this book, is to help people and organizations to be more courageous so that they can take whatever "giant leaps" they're facing. Through the work Giant Leap has done with thousands of workers and renowned organizations, we've developed a track record of helping people to be more courageous at work. Keep in mind that Giant Leap's clients are not people who have been endowed with some superhuman courage gene. Rather, they are everyday people like you and me, who choose to apply what I call *everyday courage*. That is, a more tempered and measured courage than people typically associate with courageous acts. As someone who once found courage only in adrenaline-pumping and spine-tingling situations, I can now say unequivocally that courage is not limited to extreme feats of bravery. The most important lesson my clients have taught me is this: Courage is accessible to everyone. Not just the daredevils among us.

Fear, as this book will argue, is an invitation to experience your own courage. I am a very fearful guy. But I'm also a guy who hates being controlled—by people, situations, and most of all fear. Courage, to me, beats the alternative: letting other things dictate my actions. So, whenever possible, and when operating out of my better nature, I choose courage. And when I do, I feel good about myself. This is how it is for most workers too. Workers get pumped with pride when they overcome things that are hard, challenging, and scary . . . when they take worthwhile "high dives." As a manager, when you build people's courage, you also stretch their capabilities, boost their performance, and help them to encounter their better selves. Once workers experience the value of being courageous, they begin to respond to work challenges that they formerly found frightening with newfound clarity, confidence, and conviction.

»

When you help workers to become more courageous, you stretch their capabilities, boost their performance, and help them to encounter their better selves.

»

Fear They Lose ... and So Do You

Given the benefits to be gained when workers are courageous, it's striking to me that so many managers still resort
to stoking people's fears to get things done. Managers who
fill people with fear in order to motivate them often do so
for reasons of efficiency and immaturity. It simply takes less
time, thought, and technique to bark an order than it does
to motivate people according to their interests, passion, and
capabilities. Some managers justify their behavior with excuses like "I'm too busy to coddle people" and "I'm paid to get
results, not to be nice to people." The way they see it, encouragement is a waste of time.

Having seen the wreckage caused by fear-based managers, I am convinced that fear is bad for business. Workers have a way of acting in their own worst interests when
managers overload them with fear. Like flailing about at
the sight of a bee, thinking that the best way to keep from
getting stung is to wave hysterically, the actions of workers
who are managed with fear are often dramatic and disproportionate to the fear being faced. Fear makes workers clam
up, restricting the flow of feedback that is so necessary for
keeping managers from making bonehead decisions. Fear
heightens workers' suspicions of one another, undermining
the trust that interpersonal relationships need to flourish.
Fear causes workers to be unduly preoccupied with safety,
strangling their willingness to take risks and extend their
skills. Fear lowers morale, damages relationships, erodes
trust, and builds resentment. Ultimately, fear lowers confidence, standards, and profits.

Encouragement does, as fear-stoking managers argue, take time. But providing encouragement to workers is an investment of time, not a waste of it. Don't think so? Consider the results I would have gotten if, to expedite the process of motivating Dustin Webster to do his high dive, I had used a fear-based management approach. First, I would have made him spend less time doing all those silly lead-ups. Why bother jumping off the side of the pool deck when the goal is to do a hundred-foot dive, right? I would have made sure that Dustin focused on all the things he was doing wrong so that he would stop doing them. Those were the risks, after all, that needed to be prevented. Then I would have pointed my finger in Dustin's face and told him what was at stake for the team, and me, if he screwed up. Saying this would clarify where the fault would reside if he wiped out. And instead of bothering to help Dustin to see that this dive was the next logical extension of his skills and capabilities, I would have told him that whether or not he wanted to do the dive was irrelevant—doing it was his *job*! All the while, I would have hovered over him, harping about how little time was left to get the job done.

Now, what kind of results do you think I would have gotten if I had tried to motivate Dustin by filling him with fear? Would my approach have made Dustin more confident, courageous, and optimistic? Would it have deepened his commitment to both me and the team? Would it have caused him to want to do bigger dives for me in the future? More to the bottom line, would my approach have enhanced his chances of taking a successful dive? No. In all likelihood, Dustin would have wiped out, or worse.

Your Choice—and Opportunity

As a manager, you may be tempted to resort to stoking people's fear when they aren't getting things done. Maybe this was the approach your bosses used on you. If you aim to build people's courage, however, you won't get there by putting fear inside them. You'll get there by filling workers with enough courage that they can dominate their fears. And the rewards are worth it. Workers who are courage-led are more engaged, committed, optimistic, loyal, and change-embracing. Why wouldn't they be? Imagine working for a boss whose vision was so bold that it actually excited you. Imagine working for a manager who valued mistake making as a natural and necessary part of your professional development. Imagine working for a manager who actually saw ass kissing as a repulsive, manipulative, and dishonest thing. Then go a step further and imagine what the whole company might look like if all the managers led by putting courage into their workers. It would be a workplace where you could implicitly trust the motives and intentions of everyone around you, and where you could speak the unvarnished truth without fear, and where you would make more forward-falling mistakes in order to better serve the company (and clients). This is the kind of company that Giant Leap is dedicated to creating: the courageous company.

An Alternative to Fear-Based Management

As you'll soon learn, there are better ways to use fear than threatening workers. In fact, you can harness fear's energy in ways that cause people to do courageous things. Later in the book, you'll learn why you don't have to resort to using fear just to get people to do challenging things. A far better and more impactful approach is to inspire people by helping them to find their courage. In the chapters that follow, you'll learn about four techniques for influencing people to be more courageous at work. Together, these things constitute what I call the *Courage Foundation Model* (see page 28).

Communities of Courage

My hope is that as you progress through the book, and as you start going to work with more courage, others will want to share the journey with you. There is strength in numbers. It's easier to do courageous things when you know that other people are doing them, too. When I was a high diver, for example, there was a strong feeling that we were all in it together. These days, I get the same feeling of communal support with my whitewater kayaking buddies here in Asheville. When paddling through treacherous whitewater, having the encouragement of your fellow river rats is more important than having a good boat. It makes it much easier to face an intimidating rapid when you know your buddies are there to save you if you get into a hairy situation. Similarly, when courage goes to work with each and every worker, the capacity of the entire organization to take on greater challenges is enlarged. Like ever-expanding concentric circles, every single act of courage at work has the potential to transform the business in unexpected ways. All it takes is someone to start the first ripple. As you'll learn in the next chapter, role modeling is the first and most powerful way of getting others to put their courage to work.

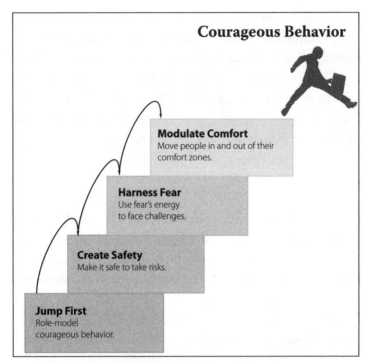

Figure 1.   The Courage Foundation Model

Jump First: Good managers are good role models. Before helping workers to be more courageous, you'll need to be more courageous yourself. Doing so allows you to get firsthand experience with the challenges you're asking workers to face and is the best way to build credibility with your direct reports.

Create Safety: Workers play it safe when it isn't safe to not play it safe. Therefore, to get them to do more courageous things, you'll need to weave safety nets that give them a sense of security as they work. You'll also have to value *forward-falling* mistakes, particularly if the lessons gleaned from those mistakes advance the team's goals.

Harness Fear: Fear in the workplace is inevitable. Your job is to make fear useful by putting it to work for you—not by threatening workers, but by building up their capacity to be courageous. Fear's energy can be used as fuel to help people to do courageous things.

Modulate Comfort: When it comes to career development, too much comfort can be a dangerous thing. As a manager, you'll need to provide comfortable workers with work challenges that make them uncomfortable and keep them motivated. At the same time, if they become too uncomfortable, you'll need to let them settle in long enough to gain confidence with their newfound skills.

Questions for Reflection

How might your team benefit if everyone started showing up to work with more courage?

_____

_____

_____

How might your career benefit if the people you lead were working more courageously?

_____

_____

_____

How would you manage differently if you prized courage above all other business virtues?

_____

_____

_____

Chapter 2

Jumping First

Each person must live their life as a role model for others.

Rosa Parks

High divers are a crazy bunch, quite comfortable doing uncomfortable and unnatural things—after all, if we were meant to fly, God would have given us wings. But despite our willingness to take unnatural leaps, one particular high-dive opportunity held little appeal for any of us. The team had been asked to perform during the annual Osmond Family Fourth of July extravaganza at Brigham Young Stadium in Provo, Utah. We were part of a lineup that included Donny and Marie, the rest of the Osmond family, singer Crystal Gayle, and actor Mr. T. More than fifty thousand spectators were expected to attend the show.

In addition to our performing a sensational repertoire

of Olympic-style dives, the entire extravaganza was to cul-
minate in a huge fireworks display as a high diver plunged
from the top of the ladder while holding two lit flares, one
in each hand. The dive was to be performed to "The Flight of
the Bumble Bee," the frenetic musical piece from the opera
Tsar Sultan. But there was a little problem. Unbeknownst to
the Osmond family, none of us bigshot divers wanted to do
the spectacular crescendo dive. First of all, the dive would be
done in the glare of a blinding spotlight after all the other
stadium lights were shut off. Second, diving with two lit flares
would severely limit the diver's arm movement, something
that is critical for performing aerial acrobatics. Finally, having to dive among all the exploding pyrotechnics presented
dangers beyond reason. The thought of getting blown up by
an errant skybomb was less than inviting.

After growing annoyed with everyone's bellyaching,
our most seasoned veteran, Hamilton Riddle, volunteered to
do it. To appreciate the magnitude of this gesture, you have
to know Hamilton. At six-foot-five and 240 pounds, Hamilton is a Goliath of a man. Because the diving tank was only
ten feet deep, Hamilton wouldn't have much stopping room.
And though he was incredibly fit, "H" (as we called him), at
forty-five years old, was the oldest eagle in our flock.

Through the rose-colored glasses of hindsight, it is
tempting to view Hamilton's volunteering to do the dive as
having something to do with his having larger *cojones* than
the rest of us. The more accurate truth is that he had more
to lose in not doing the dive. Hamilton was a part owner of
the production company that was responsible for staging the
high-diving show, and a lot of his own money was at stake.
The Osmonds had forked over a healthy sum for the show,

and now it was up to us to deliver. What choice did Hamilton really have but to step up? Courage, in this case, had more to do with desperation than with bravery. The risk of losing all that Osmond money was bigger than the risk of doing the stunt dive.

The dramatic moment when the spotlight illuminated Hamilton atop the ladder will always stay with me. There he was, this colossus of a man, arms outstretched to the sides like some mythic aerial savior, fireworks exploding all around him, perched at the top of the world. For a brief moment, Hamilton wasn't Hamilton. He had morphed into high diving's senior-most archangel. His spectacular flare dive was glorious and humbling to behold. The crowd erupted with a huge applause as he surfaced the water, fists raised in triumph. At once he represented all that each diver could have been and all that we had declined to be. Desperate or not, Hamilton had stepped up when we had backed down. He had led, courageously, by Jumping First.

Management by Jumping First

In the grand scheme of things, there are two ways to get workers to do things: push from behind or attract from the front. Managers who choose the former stand far from the battle lines, issuing directives for workers to execute. Managers who choose the latter stand on the front lines, indeed in front of the front lines, leading through the power of attraction. This is what I call *Management by Jumping First* (MBJF), and it is the most powerful and effective way of getting com-*fear*table workers to do uncomfortable things.

Courage is relative. Just as a lens can be used to

magnify or shrink an object depending on the way it is held, your perception of a situation can change dramatically based on how close to the situation you are. There is a vast difference, for example, between the perspectives of a high diver and the spectators in the audience. From the audience's vantage point peering up, the big ladder stretches up a hundred feet. But from the diver's perspective looking at the pool, it plunges a thousand feet down. The audience sits comfortably in their seats, imagining what the diver must be going through. The diver, however, isn't imagining anything. Instead, he is perched atop a rickety steel ladder, shivering from the cold wind, struggling to contain intense feelings of fear while simultaneously concentrating on the dive. In a moment, after all, he will be careening toward the pool at over fifty miles per hour protected only by a bathing suit.

The most practical reason for Jumping First is that it gives you a firsthand understanding about the risks you're asking your workers to take and, therefore, the amount of courage they'll need to meet the challenges. By experiencing the jump before they do, you'll be able to anticipate the aspects of the challenge that workers are likely to balk at. Just as important, by being the first up and off the high-dive ladder, you'll gain a lot of credibility with them. In the same way that workers have no respect for distant managers who abide by a do-as-I-say-not-as-I-do philosophy, they hold the highest respect for managers who do the uncomfortable things they are asking others to do, first.

> **Workers have the highest regard for managers who do the same uncomfortable things they are asking the workers to do, but who do them first.**
>

The word *lead* implies to *stay out in front.* As a practical reality, you cannot follow someone who is not in front of you. Jumping First involves a mixture of leadership, role modeling, and initiative, and the best way to get people to follow you is to first take the high dives you're asking others to take. Hamilton Riddle's skyrocketing dive, for example, motivated all of us divers to work harder. After the Osmond show, we had to stay up all night tearing down the equipment so that we could set it all up again in time to perform a set of shows in Saskatoon, Canada, forty-eight hours later. Hamilton's lead in stepping up and doing the big scary dive made it easier for us to deal with the fatigue of an all-night tear-down. We owed it to him to do a good job. Without Hamilton's role modeling, I'm not sure we would have worked through the night without complaining.

MBJF at Work

I once saw MBJF in action during my involvement as a facilitator of a cultural-transformation effort at a large Southern utilities organization. The company's future hinged on its ability to unleash the entrepreneurial spirit of its three-thousand-person workforce, and the entire organization was being required to attend an intensive three-day off-site culture-change program to support the endeavor. The senior managers knew that if they could get the employees to make more tactical on-the-spot decisions themselves, it would free up the managers' time so that they could focus their attention on more strategic matters. But as employees of a utility company, workers weren't used to being "entrepreneurial." So, from a cultural standpoint the behavioral transformation that the company desired of the workforce was substantial.

Leading up to the three-day off-site was a 360-degree feedback survey that gauged people's commitment to the company's newly created core values, one of which was "We make bold decisions." In true MBJF fashion, the senior managers insisted on being the first ones to subject themselves to the scrutiny of the survey. These managers weren't spectators watching their workers take high dives; instead they became high divers themselves. They didn't have to imagine why anyone might find the process uncomfortable; instead they were personally discomforted by it. Having your leadership evaluated by your boss, peers, and coworkers is enough to heighten the self-consciousness of even the most thick-skinned executive.

Because the anonymity and confidentiality of the survey respondents are assured, people are often far more candid than they would be giving feedback directly to the leader's face. By being the first to open themselves up to the scrutiny of others, the senior managers helped to motivate the rest of the workforce to get behind the changes. Their actions sent a strong message about courage and integrity—namely, that no one in the company should be exempt from the evaluation of others, most especially the company leaders. Moreover, by employing MBJF, the senior managers role-modeled their own deep commitment to the culture-change effort that they were expecting everyone else to support.

Clarifying the Views

There has been a lot written about the importance of vision to being a good leader. It's important to managers too. Managers, like leaders, need to provide workers with an inspiring vision of how better things will be (for the workers themselves and for the company) as a result of their work. But it's also important that you provide concrete "views"—smaller and more personalized visions that enable workers, at an individual level, to have a clear line of sight between their efforts and their advancement. To do that, you'll need to stand on the same high-dive ladders that you're asking workers to stand on. This doesn't mean you have to have the very same skills as they do. Rather, it means having firsthand experience with challenges that are similar to those you're asking them to face. So, if you're expecting a worker to go through the nerve-racking experience of making a presentation to the senior executive team, you should have had that experience somewhere along the line, too. Likewise, if you're asking a worker to take a hard-line position with a vendor, or deal with an angry customer, or lead a death-march project, you should have faced similar challenges as part of your career at some point, too.

Too often, managers are seen as mouthpieces of the higher-ups. This is validated for workers when you mimic the same phrases that every other executive uses. When lower-level employees hear you talk about the "strategic value-added proposition for the end-users," for example, they start to think that you've drunk too much of the organizational happy-juice. When workers come to think of you as little more than an executive parrot, any vision you offer them becomes suspect. By Jumping First, you inspire workers to value you as an independent thinker. They see that the vision you hold is grounded in real work experiences and an authentic desire to see them succeed. Jumping First helps you to create individual *views* that each respective worker can use to succeed—

views that are more specific, concrete, and easier to follow than a large abstract vision. Providing workers with narrower and clearly defined views, based on your own firsthand experiences of what they are contending with, is far more useful to them in their daily work lives than trumpeting an ethereal company vision that will take years to materialize.

Jumping with Attitude

By Jumping First, you set an attitudinal and behavioral tone that others learn to emulate. It helps to lead not from where people are, but from where you need them to be. To this end, it is useful to identify the attitudes and behaviors you find frustrating, and then be sure to role-model opposite ones. If, for example, your direct reports are apathetic, you should counterbalance their apathy by being energetic. The idea here is that as a manager you shouldn't expect workers to be held to a standard by which you don't abide. Thus if you want workers to show more initiative, you first must show initiative. If you want them to go out of their way to understand how their work connects to a broader vision, or to have more accountability for their work, or to be more positive, you must do these things first.

Going to work with your own courage will go a long way toward getting others to go to work with theirs.

Jumping First . . . First

In the last chapter, you were introduced to the Courage Foundation Model, which depicts four things you'll need to do in order to get people to be more courageous. Most often, Jumping First, doing what you're asking others to do, is the most powerful part of the model. It requires you to focus on you before focusing on them. Before figuring out how to get people to have the courage to demonstrate more initiative, trust, and assertiveness, first figure out how you're going to do those things. Nothing is as powerful as role-modeling the courageous behavior you expect from others.

Here are some questions that will help you to Manage by Jumping First:

Questions for Reflection

As a manager, what are some ways that you have been too com*fear*table? What might your own actions, attitudes, or behaviors be transmitting to your workers?

_____

_____

_____

What kind of role model are you for courageous behavior? What could you do to be a better courage role model?

_____

_____

_____

Think about each worker you're responsible for. What challenging experiences have you faced in your career that might be useful to them? How might these experiences help you to develop "views" for each of them?

_____

_____

_____

What behaviors or attitudes do you find frustrating about your direct reports? What compensatory behaviors or attitudes should you start role-modeling in order to help shift their behavior?

_____

_____

_____

Chapter 3

Create Safety Nets

Safety first . . . because accidents last.

Unknown

Over the years, a lot of people have inspired me with their courage. But none as much as my four-year-old daughter, Tobina. Bina, as we call her, has cerebral palsy. She is also profoundly deaf. Both challenges are the byproducts of a virulent staph infection she contracted at the hospital just days after she was born.

Americans with disabilities make up the largest minority population in the United States. Some 54 million Americans have a disability of one form or another. And anyone who has been graced by the company of such people knows what a blessing it can be. It can also be heartbreaking. During Bina's first year, it became clear that she was lagging behind her twin brother, Alex, in significant ways. Alex rolled over. Bina didn't. Alex crawled. Bina didn't. Alex responded to our baby talk. Bina didn't. Alex received adoring smiles from strangers. Bina didn't.

At first, all I could focus on was Bina's disabilities, which caused me a lot of anger. I'd think, "Why did this happen to her? Who caused this?" and "Why can't she do the things her brother can do?" Then, just before she turned two, a friend of mine wisely suggested that I start focusing on Bina's abilities, not her disabilities. When I heeded my friend's advice, Bina started progressing much more rapidly. In some strange way, my anger had become a block to Bina's progress. Looking back, I suspect that I had begun to pigeonhole Bina as "handicapped" and in subtle ways was treating her as such.

One summer a few months before Bina's fourth birthday, I set up a trampoline in the backyard in a not-so-subtle effort to nudge Alex toward springboard diving. On afternoons when I wasn't on the road, I'd bounce on the trampoline with Alex and teach him tricks. Bina would be there too, laughing and watching us from the corner of the trampoline bed. At the end of our practice sessions I'd always make time for Bina too, holding her little hands and bouncing up and down.

One day, just to see what would happen, I sat behind Bina, stood her upright, steadied her hips, and let go of her hands. Then my little girl did something she never had done before: She took three full steps. On the hard floor, Bina was never confident enough to do this. Kids with cerebral palsy fall down a lot, and Bina was no different. She had fallen off enough chairs to know that the hard floor wasn't her friend. So watching Bina take three teetering steps was hugely thrilling. On her fourth step she fell to the mat and giggled as my wife, Shannon, and I cheered wildly.

Recognizing that we were onto something, Shannon and I began to set aside time each day to walk with Bina on the trampoline. Before long, three steps turned to five steps, and five turned into ten. Then we set up a long runner of matted cushion on our back deck, figuring it would help her make the transition from the spongy trampoline surface to the hardwood floor. Drawing on her trampoline successes, Bina cautiously stepped out on the runner. Soon she was taking more steps on the deck than she was able to on the trampoline. It was all terrifically encouraging and inspiring. Here was our daughter taking her first awkward steps, courageously and persistently . . . at four years old.

Bina eventually graduated to walking on our hardwood floors. Now she even walks on our concrete driveway. Walking unaided has helped her to become more self-reliant and confident. Though Bina isn't running circles around us yet, Shannon and I believe that soon she will be. The transformation we've witnessed in Bina's willingness to take the risk of walking has been nothing short of astounding, teaching us the value of creating safety as a way of enabling courageous behavior in our brave little girl.

Safety First

By setting up our backyard trampoline, we had inadvertently stumbled upon a safe way for Bina to do something that she had previously felt was too unsafe to do. Walking, formerly a frightening and potentially injuring experience, now had become fun. Notice that the action we wanted Bina to take (walking) hadn't changed. What had changed was the consequence (and only temporarily). The spongy trampoline surface was far more forgiving than our hardwood floors. When we surrounded the same action with safer consequences, Bina became much more willing to take a risk.

» The safer people feel, the more risks they are likely to take. People extend themselves when the consequences for doing so are forgiving. »

In the same way that increasing Bina's safety by reducing the negative consequences encouraged her to take the risk of walking, workers will be much more likely to step up to challenges when there are safety nets in place. People take risks relative to how safe they feel. The more forgiving the consequences, the more likely people are to extend themselves. This does not mean that getting people to be courageous means creating a risk-free environment. Rather, it means supporting their courageous actions with a reasonable amount of safety.

At work, setting up safety nets is essential for promoting courageous behavior. For example, I once worked with an executive who was asked to head up a new division in a totally new market. Accepting the job meant also accepting considerable risk. For one, he would have to move out of his leadership role in one of the company's established and successful divisions. The new role meant that, at least for a little while, he'd have fewer employees, fewer resources, and potentially less stature in the company. It was possible that his colleagues would come to view him as leading the company's pet experiment. Worse yet, his colleagues might view the new division as a "special project" and start suspecting that the move was little more than a kind way of putting the executive out to pasture. To offset these risks, the owner of the company created a number of safety nets. First, he supported the new undertaking with a significant infusion of capital. The money would help cover the high costs of new market entry and prevent the executive from being in the impossible position of creating something out of nothing. Second, on numerous occasions the owner personally championed the effort, making everyone aware that creating the new division was a top strategic priority. Finally, he promoted the executive—*before* the executive had formally moved into the role. This showed people, tangibly and symbolically, that not only was the executive not being put out to pasture, but he was now going to have even more clout and influence.

Such safety nets didn't remove the risk of failure. Nor did they reduce the amount of work it would require to make the new division successful. Instead, the safety nets supported the executive by showing him the confidence the organization had in his ability to be successful. The company had his back. The safety nets made launching a new division more attractive, and less risky, to the executive. With safety nets in place, it was easier for the executive to be courageous and accept the new role.

Don't Look Down!

Too many managers fixate on magnifying the consequences of failure instead of building safety nets that promote success. They spend far too much time reminding people about the consequences if things go wrong instead of clarifying what things will look like if they go right. They say such things as, "Whatever you do, don't screw up!" and "If you drop the ball

》
You can't be critical and encouraging at the same time. Paying too much attention to "all the things that can go wrong" draws focus away from all the things you need to get right.
》

on this, you're toast!" Such things are akin to telling a diver not to wipe out instead of how to nail the dive.

Many people get promoted into the management ranks because of their critical-thinking skills, particularly in industries like consulting, engineering, and technology. Such skills allow for accurate problem solving. Critical-thinking skills also help uncover flaws and help mitigate, minimize, and control risks. The danger occurs, however, when critical thinkers place a disproportionate amount of attention on "all the things that can go wrong." It is difficult, if not downright impossible, for a manager to be simultaneously critical and encouraging. By placing too much emphasis on criticism, the manager draws too much of the workers' attention to the things that must be avoided. When all of the attention is being paid to what can go wrong, too little attention is given to how to make things go right. By focusing solely on the consequences of failure, such managers are, in effect, widening the holes in the safety nets. When managers continuously obsess about all the bad things that must be avoided, they end up injecting workers with so much anxiety that it creates an untenable amount of performance pressure, undermining their confidence and creating, ironically, an unsafe situation.

Three Ways to Build Safety Nets

If your aim is to help people to be more courageous, you'd be wise to create safety nets. And because safety (and danger) occurs on many levels, weaving tight nets requires a multifaceted approach. For some, safety comes in the form of financial stability. Such people will risk doing courageous things to the extent that those risks don't jeopardize their job security. For others, safety has more to do with preserving their reputation. They will take risks as long as doing so won't make them look bad. Still others find safety in belonging to a group. They will do courageous things as long as their place in the community isn't threatened. As a manager, you'll find that gaining a clear understanding of each worker's definition of safety will help you to craft each person's net. That said, there are three specific ways of building safety nets regardless of which kind of safety is involved:

- Give people permission to be courageous.

- Value forward-falling mistakes.

- Provide air cover.

Giving Permission to Be Courageous

Often the most powerful action you can take to provoke courageous behavior is to give people permission to be courageous. Before starting my own company, I worked for Accenture, one of the world's largest and most respected management and technology consulting companies, as its first-ever internal executive coach. Before moving into the coaching role, however, I remember being petrified at the prospect of coaching the senior executives whom I worked with. As a middle manager, I had reported to a few of them and knew how intimidating some of them were. I feared that my lower rank would cause my coaching guidance to be discounted and that eventually my role would be marginalized. Nearly all of the senior execs had more business experience than I had, yet I'd be counseling them. Safety for me meant preserving the positive reputation I had built up prior to that moment. Moving into the new coaching role, I feared, might threaten it.

I was so worried about failing that I strongly considered forgoing the opportunity, despite the fact that I wanted it badly. Now, admitting to your boss that you're scared of failing is hard to do in any company. It is particularly hard to do in a company made up of hotshot consultants. But I was fortunate to be working for Hines Brannan, a seasoned and level-headed senior partner. Hines had a way of lifting my head up past the speed bumps of the moment so that I could view my career as a winding journey. So I went to him and said, "Hines, I think you should consider placing someone else in the new coaching role. I'm okay with coaching people at my level, but it wouldn't be fair for me to coach people who are more senior than me. I mean, I've reported to some of these people in the past. The thought of coaching them is just too intimidating."

Hines listened patiently. Then, instead of telling me what a wuss I was being, he simply said, "But Bill, you coach me."

He was right. Like many of the senior executives I would be coaching, I reported to him. And over the years, I had become a bit of a confidant to him. In the process, I had grown comfortable offering Hines my perspective on issues and challenges that he was grappling with. I'm sure that Hines had far more impact on me as a coach than I ever had on him, but in the moments when I had coached him, he had drawn value from it. By pointing out the obvious, Hines gave me permission to see the opportunity in a different way. The confidence I had already established in coaching him could be extended to working with the other executives. His words helped me to cut myself a break. Moreover, his words helped put my courage to work. After all, if I could coach the most senior executive on the account, certainly I could coach the people who reported to him.

The most important thing that Hines did was to give me permission to express my fears without embarrassment. Unlike some bosses I had worked for, Hines didn't make me feel small so that he could feel big. With him, I never felt dismissed or patronized. He never disrespected me by multitasking when I talked with him, despite his pressing schedule. To the contrary, when I approached him, I always had his full presence and attention. I felt valued, not intimidated. Because Hines's disposition permitted me to express myself without fear, when I did, he was in a much better position to provide me with good counsel. Had I reported to another executive, I would have been much more reluctant to express my fears and concerns.

More tangibly, Hines gave me permission to be courageous by pointing out where I was already doing the very thing I was afraid of. This was incontrovertible proof that I could indeed meet the challenge . . . because I was already meeting it. Armed with this knowledge, I was able to build up a thriving internal coaching practice, eventually coaching thirty Accenture executives on a regular basis.

Permission enhances safety. Often workers avoid doing courageous things because their heads are telling them that they aren't "allowed" to. As a manager, how you carry yourself will make a big impact on how safe they feel and, thus, on how expressive they will be. By giving them your full presence, you'll cause them to feel valued and "allowed" to bring their fears out in the open. When they do, you'll be better able to address their concerns and shift their thinking to all the ways they are prepared to meet their challenges.

Valuing "Forward-Falling" Mistakes

EarthLink, one of Giant Leap's first clients, tells its employees that there is a big difference between good mistakes (best effort, bad results) and bad mistakes (sloppiness or lack of effort). Such messages help inspire EarthLink's workers to have the courage to be innovative. The managers in many other companies we've worked with, unfortunately, hold a more restrictive view, seeing all mistakes as bad ones. They get equally upset regardless of whether mistakes are made honestly or carelessly.

Not all mistakes are created equal, and wise managers know that not making any mistakes is just as dangerous as making too many. I once gave a talk on courage to three hundred sales executives from BellSouth Small Business Services (now part of AT&T). Prior to the talk, I spoke with David Scobey, the company president, to get his perspective on risk taking and the necessity of mistake making. He said, "Mistakes are critically important to growth. Not just individually but collectively as well. Growth is driven by innovation, and innovation often comes from making the right mistakes. As long as the mistakes aren't habitual, and as long as they key us onto something we hadn't known before, then they're worth making. In my mind I have a mistake ratio, and always strive to achieve the right balance between not making any mistakes and making too many. Either condition will hurt the business."

When your people know that you value smart and nonhabitual mistakes, they become more willing to do courageous things. The trick is to define what a good mistake is. One of our clients conducts monthly "lessons learned" breakfasts, each attended by more than one hundred project managers. During the sessions, project mistakes are highlighted and the team responsible for making the mistake does the presenting! But the focus is never on punishing or embarrassing the mistake makers. Instead, the focus is on the lessons learned that can be gleaned from the mistake, and on creating a higher standard of professionalism that can be applied across the business. The meetings have taught people that mistakes are a normal and necessary part of business, as long as the mistakes are put to good use for the company.

As a manager, you have to be willing to let people scrape their knees a little. By allowing them to make their own mistakes and not berating them when they do, you create a safety net that allows them to be more experimental and innovative.

Providing Air Cover

The job of a middle manager is sometimes like being on a medieval torture rack. You're pulled at one end by the demands of your bosses, and at the other by the needs of your direct reports. It's a tough place to be, because your bosses sign your paycheck but your people determine your success.

More often than not, though, managers pay more attention to their bosses than to their employees. Having administered scores of 360-degree feedback appraisals, I can tell you definitely that middle managers are far more likely to "manage up" than "manage down."

Workers have favoritism radar and are keenly sensitive to the inequitable behavior of their managers. What are they to think, for example, when you spend far more time with your boss than you do with them? Or how about when you cut them off in mid-sentence and start responding to your boss's BlackBerry message? Why, they wonder, do you answer your boss's cell phone calls on the first ring, but their calls go straight to voice mail? Such behavior on your part signals to workers that you lack confidence. After all, what kind of confidence can you have when you possess all the composure of a frightened puppy when responding to senior executive requests? Taken further, workers start to wonder how effective you are at pushing back when the boss's requests become unreasonable, such as when your boss demands that a deadline be accelerated, forcing workers to unexpectedly work nights and weekends.

While workers recognize the legitimate need for you to be responsive to your boss's demands, they lose confidence in you if you respond impulsively to executive requests without considering the impact that those requests may have on them. Your decisions impact their lives. When they can't trust with any degree of certainty that commitments you make to them won't soon be broken by even the most random of executive requests, they start feeling like objects, not people. Worse, they stop respecting you. Why should they? You aren't respecting them.

Workers will be more courageous when they see you being more courageous toward your bosses. Workers want to know that you're courageous enough to stick up for them and provide them with a safety net of "air cover." They want to know that you'll go to bat for them when they are overworked, or underresourced, or burned out. They want to feel that they matter, too, and that their needs are considered when decisions that impact them are being made. When they know that you can confidently express their concerns to your bosses, they feel that you have their back and that they have a voice in the decision-making process. When you are as consistently attentive to their needs as you are to your bosses', workers respond to truly urgent requests with much more gusto. Moreover, when workers see you interacting with your bosses with confidence and courage, it becomes safer (and easier) for them to be confident and courageous when they interact with you.

Go Safely

It is easier for workers to be courageous when you create safety nets. Increased safety lessens fear and increases workers' willingness to carry out uncomfortable tasks. The height of the dive is determined by the depth of the pool. Likewise, the more substantial the risk you're asking workers to take, the more safety nets you'll have to put in place.

Keep in mind that it is rarely possible and often counterproductive to remove all danger from challenging situations. Regardless of how tightly woven the safety nets you've constructed are, there will still be holes in them, and those remaining holes will inspire fear. The next step in the Courage Foundation Model deals with how to harness fear. As the following chapter shows, even when there are holes in workers' safety nets, workers can still learn how to be courageous by putting fear to good use.

Questions for Reflection

What are you likely to be transmitting to your workers in the way you currently respond to your boss's demands? On balance, would they say you manage up or manage down? Would they say you're courageous in your interactions with people more senior than you? If not, what would help you to interact more courageously?

_____

_____

_____

What behaviors on your part would make workers feel allowed to be more courageous? What could you say or do to give each employee permission to be courageous?

_____

_____

_____

How do you currently handle mistakes? How would
you define a *good* mistake? What is an example of a
recent good mistake that was made on your team? In
what ways were you and your team able to capitalize on
the mistake?

_____

_____

_____

As a percentage of time, how much time do you spend
with your bosses and how much do you spend with
your direct reports? Can you provide a recent example
of when you provided air cover for one of your workers?

_____

_____

_____

Chapter 4

Harness Fear

Courage is knowing what not to fear.

Plato

*Courage is not the absence of fear, but rather the judgment
that something else is more important than fear.*

Ambrose Redmoon

*Why do some people move toward their fears, while others
move away from them?* It is precisely this question that I
grappled with during the writing of my first book, *Right Risk*.
It might surprise you to learn that a lot of authors don't write
about what they know; they write about what they *want* to
know. And I wanted to know why I chose to deal with my fear
of heights by becoming a high diver. When confronted with
fear, why did I move toward it instead of away from it?

If you judge *Right Risk* by its cover, you might draw the
inaccurate conclusion that the book is opinion-based—an
ex-athlete's lopsided treatise on the importance of risk taking. In reality, the book is quite research-based. To discover

the answer to my question, I searched out all the information I could find on subjects related to risk, fear, and courage.
Eventually I found the Rosetta stone I was looking for, and it
came from the work of Michael J. Apter.

Apter is a psychologist and the author of several books,
including a terrific tome called *Danger: Our Love of Living on
the Edge* (Oneworld Publications, 2007). A Ph.D. and visiting
professor at several major universities, Apter is best known
as the codeveloper of Reversal Theory—a motivational theory that explains why individuals often behave in contradic-
tory ways (such as why a guy who's afraid of heights becomes
a high diver!).

I was so taken with Apter's work that I tracked him
down on the Internet. After enjoying a pleasant exchange
by e-mail, I noticed his phone number at the bottom of his
message, so I gave him a call. Seemingly delighted that I had
taken such an interest in his work, he kindly offered to have
lunch with me if I was ever in the Washington, D.C., area,
where he lives. Reflecting back on it, I'm sure that he was just
being nice. But because I was hell-bent on finding out the
answer to my fear *facers* and *avoiders* question, I called Apter
again the next day and asked if I could fly up to D.C. to meet
with him. I also invited myself to stay at his house!

When I told my wife that I had invited myself to Apter's
house and that he had said yes, she shook her head, saying,
"What if this Apter guy is a serial killer with a collection of
heads in his basement?!"

Fortunately, Apter turned out to be one of the most
fascinating and generous people I've ever met—a warm, ec-
centric, and slightly disheveled British chap. Everything you'd
expect in a university professor. Apter and I spent two days

musing about the function of danger and risk in people's lives. In the process, I learned this critical secret: *All of us are both fear facers and fear avoiders*. You might have no problem at all asserting yourself to people in positions of authority. I, on the other hand, might become a tongue-tied buffoon when talking to the boss. Conversely, you might get petrified at the thought of going whitewater kayaking, something I do for sport. As discussed in the previous chapter, you'll pursue fearful situations when you perceive yourself to have at least some degree of safety, and you'll avoid them when you don't.

Caging the Tiger

The willingness to face fear hinges on what Apter calls a "protective frame." As he explained it to me, a protective frame is like a cage you can build around your fear so as to contain it. When facing a fearful situation, you can build a robust protective frame by doing such things as gathering all the facts surrounding the situation, getting mentored by others who have faced similar challenges, and acquiring the skills you'll need to competently face the task. As you strengthen your protective frame, you become capable of withstanding greater amounts of fear.

Apter explained the concept to me this way: "Think about going to a zoo and seeing an empty cage. You'd be bored out of your wits. Now imagine going to the same zoo and seeing a tiger prowling around after escaping its cage. You'd freeze with fright or you'd run like bloody hell. To convert fear into excitement, you need both a tiger and a cage. When your tiger (fear) is contained in a strong cage (protective frame), you'll enjoy the zoo!"

Protective frames are not safety nets. Safety nets are essentially about lowering workers' risks (and fear) by lessening the consequences of failure. They are about shrinking the tiger. Protective frames, on the other hand, are about increasing workers' capacity for dealing with big tigers. Protective frames have to do with backbone. Rather than reduce fear, protective frames build workers' confidence and capabilities to help them withstand, and match, the tiger's intensity. With a robust protective frame, the size of the tiger stays the same but the size of one's confidence gets bigger.

» A protective frame is a mechanism for harnessing your fear. The stronger your protective frame, the more fear you can withstand. »

Turning Fear into Fun

Protective frames allow workers to harness and transform their fear. It turns out that there is hardly any neurological difference between intense feelings of fear and intense feelings of excitement. They are known to be *neurological correlates*. Think, for example, about what happens to you when you're really afraid. Your palms sweat, your heart races, your breath gets short, and your stomach teems with butterflies. Well, guess what? Those same things happen to you when you're going to have sex! Or ride on a roller coaster, or watch a scary movie, or splash through rapids in a kayak. As far as scientists can tell, human beings are the only creatures to purposely seek out dangerous situations just for fun. But that fun is contingent upon having a strong enough internal constitution that you can withstand the fear's intensity.

Though fear and excitement are neurologically similar,

there is one critical difference between them. Fear is experienced as *displeasure* and excitement is experienced as *pleasure*. This explains why some people move toward fear and others move away. Fear facers draw at least some level of excitement (and therefore pleasure) from the situation. Simply put, people seek out situations that are pleasurable and avoid those that cause displeasure. But the key is this: What is pleasurable or displeasureable isn't determined by the situation; it's determined by the strength of the cage. When a person's confidence exceeds his fear, the feelings prompted by the situation start to skew toward pleasure. A worker who has built a strong cage (by doing such things as gathering all the facts, practicing and rehearsing, or seeking out coaching) will view a challenge far more positively than someone who hasn't. In other words, having a strong cage helps a worker to convert fear into excitement. Perhaps more important, when challenges are experienced as pleasurable, workers will start seeking them out instead of avoiding them.

For managers, one key takeaway from Apter's work is that reducing people's fear is sometimes exactly the wrong thing to focus on. When you reduce people's fear, you stand the chance of reducing their intensity as well. A better approach is to increase their confidence through preparation. When Sarah Hughes thrillingly (and unexpectedly) won the 2002 Olympic women's figure skating competition, for example, it wasn't because she reduced her fear. Rather, it was because she matched the intensity of the moment. By being exceedingly well prepared and

»

People seek out situations that cause pleasure and avoid those that don't. The stronger a person's protective frame, the more likely he or she is to experience a challenging situation as pleasurable.

»

rehearsed, she built a well-fortified cage that helped her to contain her fear. For you as a manager, when it comes to the fears of your workers, it is more important to *contain* the tigers than to *tame* them.

All of this comes back to courage and the critical question I had posed to Michael Apter: *Why do some people face their fears and others avoid them?* People face their fears when they have enough internal strength, in the form of physical and psychological preparedness, to view the experience as enjoyable.

Three Ways to Harness Fear

The goal of harnessing fear is putting fear's energy to good use. Fear, like electricity, can be paralyzing. But properly harnessed, it can provide workers with the energy they'll need to sustain them when facing challenging situations. Here are three things you can do to get the most out of fear:

- Normalize it.

- Tie it to courage.

- Use its energy.

Normalizing Fear

Worse than fear is its emotional corollary, shame. Workers, particularly men, feel embarrassed about feeling fearful. When comparing themselves with more confident coworkers, fearful workers see themselves as inadequate, wondering, "What's wrong with me that I can't be more fearless?" When shame enters the room, confidence walks out the door.

In dealing with fearful workers, it is tempting to want to

discount their fears by telling them, "Don't be afraid." But doing so is silly and ineffective. They *are* afraid. So why not acknowledge that instead? Acknowledging fear makes it more ordinary, lessening workers' feelings of shame. "Of course you're afraid," you might say, "why wouldn't you be?"

During Giant Leap's courage-building workshops, we often include a segment where each participant shares a fear that he or she is facing at work. The ensuing conversations are rich and profound, and for me the most important and gratifying aspects of our work. Fear, when exposed to the light of day, loses its potency. When workers voice their fears, the fears become more normal and mundane. These conversations, which often last a few hours, help mitigate workers' feelings of shame because they begin to realize that at any moment nearly all people are dealing with some type of work-related fear. By far the most common thing participants tell me after these conversations is that by hearing the fears of their coworkers, they feel "less screwed up" than they did before the workshop. The fact that so many people are contending with a workplace fear shows them that fear is a normal part of the work experience. Once workers start to see fear as normal, they give it less attention, which allows them to shift their focus away from it.

Tie Fear to Courage

Many people wrongly exclude fear from the definition of courage, believing that courage is the absence of fear. Every time such people feel afraid, they assume that they aren't courageous. The reality, though, is that courage is fear*ful*. When we are acting courageously, we are, most typically, very afraid. But we don't allow the fear we're carrying to stop us.

Instead, we press on. This is the signature feature of courage: to carry on despite being fearful. Fear, thus, is an essential element in the definition of courage. You can't be courageous unless you are afraid.

When fear is included in the definition of courage, fearful situations turn into opportunities to demonstrate courage. The best evidence that a worker is being courageous is that she shows all the signs of being afraid but is taking action anyway. The worker whose voice shakes when giving a presentation to the senior team, but who presses on despite being afraid, is being courageous. So is the nervous worker who informs you immediately after making a mistake. Likewise the worker who risks her job by giving you feedback, politely but bluntly, that nobody else had the guts to give you. People who press on despite being full of fear epitomize what it means to be courageous. This is exactly the type of behavior that you as a manager want to acknowledge and reinforce. Few things stiffen the spine with pride as much as hearing your boss say things like "I'm impressed with how courageous you're being" or "Thanks for being so courageous."

Great careers are defined by courageous moments. Read the biography of any prominent business figure and you'll inevitably come across a defining moment that hinged on courageously facing a fear. Workers need to be reminded that any professional worth his salt will be tested by fear-provoking situations. Such situations become invitations for workers to discover their own mettle. This point was brought home to me during a talk I once attended by Rudy Giuliani, the former mayor of New York City. He was reflecting on the lessons that his father had given him about courage, and how he drew on those lessons during the days immediately after 9/11. Giuliani's advice was instructive and underscores how closely courage and fear are tied together. He said, "If you don't have a fear, you'd better go get one. Dealing with fear is how you find your courage."

Use Fear's Energy

The best way to deal with fear is to use it against itself. Fear is not inert. It has energy. When properly harnessed, fear's energy can provide momentum for facing challenging situations. During Giant Leap's first year in business, we were hired to design a leadership-development program for Accenture and its largest client account. During a one-on-one interview with the senior executive responsible for the program, I asked him what was the most important leadership message he wanted to reinforce with the three hundred managers who would be going through the program. He said, "The most important thing people need to know is that leadership depends on having *sweaty palms.*"

"Huh?" I said.

He explained, "For our managers to grow, and for our account to be most successful, our managers need to regularly be doing things that are so scary for them that it causes their palms to sweat. Fear comes with challenge, and having sweaty palms shows you, physiologically, that fear is energizing the body. You get sweaty palms by moving outside of your comfort zone and into your courage zone. It's inside your courage zone where the learning and growing happens."

For workers, having sweaty palms means learning to carry fear with them when facing challenges. Again, courage is not about being fearless. It's about taking your fear with you. Part of your job as a manager is to help people to stop fearing fear. Fear is a business reality. Fear is. Harnessing fear helps workers to capitalize on fear's energy so that they can do challenging and courageous things.

Questions for Reflection

When facing challenging situations, which do you focus on more, reducing people's fear or increasing their confidence? How might you strengthen people's cages instead of trying to shrink their tigers?

_____

_____

_____

Think back to a specific moment in your career that you are particularly proud of. What role did fear play in this episode? What role did courage play? What does this tell you about the relationship between fear, courage, and challenge?

_____

_____

_____

Describe a recent sweaty-palm example of when one of your employees did something outside his or her comfort zone. How did it pan out? What lessons did your worker likely draw from the experience? What lessons did you draw?

_____

_____

_____

Chapter 5

Modulate Comfort

There are risks and costs to a program of action. But they are far less than the long-range risks and costs of comfortable inaction.

John F. Kennedy

I started my career in organizational development facilitating team-building programs. Having spent seven years as a member of the U.S. High Diving Team, I was able to incorporate my own experiences (and frustrations) as a team member into the facilitated sessions. Before long I had facilitated some five hundred team-building workshops for teams of all shapes and sizes. My experiences as a team member and as a team-building facilitator have taught me that bored teams are in far worse shape than those that are overworked. Rustout is worse than burnout when it comes to performance.

I once led a team-building workshop for an information

technology project team of a large communications company. The team was responsible for maintaining the software
of the company's antiquated billing system. As a regulated
entity, the company was ridiculously bureaucratic. The bud-
geting process alone was a nightmare. Most budgets weren't
approved until at least six months into the year for which
the budget was created. This meant that "critical" IT projects that were slated to begin in January couldn't get started
until at least July, regardless of how urgent the project. Most
project-completion dates, however, did not change. So project teams were in an impossible whiplash position. For the
first six months of the year they'd sit on their duffs. But once
the budget was approved, they'd work like firefighters at a
gas explosion. Such was the case with the team I got called in
to work with, except that I got them during the duff-sitting
period.

Now, I think I'm pretty good at what I do and always
strive to keep my clients "edutained." As someone who gets
bored easily, I am keenly aware of what it takes to keep people engaged during executive-development workshops. To
keep things interesting, I use a blended-learning approach,
which includes content "lecturettes," engaging breakouts,
and experiential problem-solving activities. But I'm here to
tell you, there was nothing I could do to spark this team out
of their funk. They were comfortable to the point of erosion.
One participant spent the session flipping through a fishing
magazine! Another fell asleep. Ouch.

Finally, I stopped what I was doing and said, "Okay,
clearly this workshop is not working for you. What gives?"

"Don't worry, man," the fisherman said, "it's not you.
We're just in our hibernation season."

The Season of Hibernation

The workers just mentioned were at the far edges of comfort. It's a place where lethargy replaces energy, avoidance replaces initiative, and apathy replaces passion. When workers start hibernating, everything slows to a crawl. Lunches linger. Conversations wander without aim. Work gets perpetually pushed off "until tomorrow." Worse, the skills and mental acuity of hibernating workers get dull. They make more mistakes (and care less when they do). As a manager, you need to know that the comfort part of the com*fear*table phenomenon is just as detrimental as fear in causing declines in performance.

The problem with comfort is that it is so danged comfortable. Comfort has a settling effect. When comfort settles in for too long, workers begin to lower their standards. They "settle" for less. They become less conscientious, less attentive, and less ambitious. Some also become less loyal. Workers who are comfortable to the point of boredom are flight risks. The more bored they are, the more likely they are to leave. At least the smart ones will. They're the ones who still have enough self-respect to pursue more challenging jobs somewhere else. The lazy ones, the ones who are too settled, will stay and bog things down.

Your job as a manager is to keep comfort from getting too comfortable.

The Zone of Discomfort

After years of research, I've yet to find out who came up with the term *comfort zone*. Whoever it was deserves credit for having coined a term that has become one of the most popularly used expressions in the English language. *Comfort zone* is used to explain everything from pleasant contentment to entrenched stubbornness. Often we use the term to spur workers toward greater growth and development, such as when we encourage them to "stretch" their comfort zone. Other times we use the term derisively, like when we complain about working fossils who are so encrusted in their own ways that they lack the guts to move beyond the confines of what they know. Such people, we say, are "stuck" inside their comfort zone.

Comfort is something we simultaneously (and contradictorily) strive for and guard against. We talk about performing better within our zone of comfort, but we also know that if we become too comfortable, our skills start to curdle like expired milk. Thus comfort ranges on a continuum between contentment and apathy, the former bringing strong feelings of security and the latter prompting feelings of resignation and defeat. After a while, comfort can become very uncomfortable. The silver lining: The more discomfort that comfort causes, the more likely we are to change and, potentially, grow.

The key for you as a manager is to modulate between comfort and discomfort by intensifying and de-intensifying the work challenges you parcel out to your staff. When they are nestled in their comfort zone, your role is to provide them with challenges that move them into a zone of *dis*comfort. When they become too uncomfortable, your role is to bring them back to a place of confidence. This modulating between comfort and discomfort is exactly the process we used as high divers to stretch our capacity for doing harder (and higher) dives.

Acrobatic dives are the skills of the diving trade. There are basic skills, called *requireds*, that all divers are required to know. Front dives and back dives, for example, are required dives. Required dives are the foundational dives that all other dives build off of. The front dive, for example, leads to a front double, which leads to a two-and-a-half, and so on all the way up to a front four-and-a-half somersault! Few divers in the world will ever perform a front four-and-a-half, but all divers will do front dives. Most divers will also eventually aspire to do dives with higher degrees of difficulty. No diver will be satisfied knowing how to do just a front dive. Once you learn that dive, your coach starts nudging you to do harder dives, which you want to do anyway. You see the other divers doing the harder dives, and you don't want to be left out. But learning more difficult dives means, at least for a little while, accepting all the discomfort that comes with it. Diving is a trial-and-error sport. Learning harder dives nearly always means doing a bunch of screaming belly whompers on your way to a new dive. Welts come with the territory. Divers struggle with a constant tension between perfecting the dives they already know and attempting new dives they've never done.

Like divers, most workers naturally aspire to learn more challenging tasks. Inherently they know that acquiring new skills is good for their careers. They know too that gaining these new skills requires doing things that are outside of their comfort zone. This is the case at pretty much every level of the organization. Even the guy sorting mail in the mailroom is eventually going to want to learn how to use the newfangled automated tracking system. Your job as a manager is to provide workers with skill-stretching assignments that have a higher

» **Your job as a manager is to provide workers with skill-stretching assignments that have a higher degree of difficulty than their current skill sets.** »

degree of difficulty than their current skill sets. That means purposely making workers uncomfortable, at least for a short period of time. Then, when they master those challenges and regain their comfort, you start the whole process all over again. In a sense, your role is compensatory to theirs. When they are comfortable, you provide discomforting challenges. When they are too uncomfortable, you let them settle in with the newly acquired skills long enough to become comfortable again. You become like a life-sized metronome regulating the intervals of time between comfort and discomfort.

The psychological dynamic at play here is called the *mere exposure effect*. The more people get "merely exposed" to the situation that is making them uncomfortable, the more desensitized to its effects they become, until they become comfortable again. What starts out as uncomfortable eventually becomes comfortable. When it does, people become capable of being exposed to even greater discomfort.

Notice that there's more being modulated than comfort. You're also modulating the amount of courage that people are using. Each time you expose people to greater levels of discomfort and each time you intensify the challenges they face, you are, *de facto*, causing them to be more courageous.

Methods of Modulation

To *modulate* means to vary the frequency or volume of a thing. As it relates to workers, you're varying the intensity of the challenges they face (and thus the comfort they feel). With that in mind, here are three ways of modulating comfort:

- Answer the *Holy Question*.

- Provide energy-creating challenges.

- Practice lead-ups.

Answer the Holy Question

It's funny—in all my years as a consultant, I've never heard a front-line worker say, "I can't wait to make more money for our shareholders today!" It doesn't matter what your company peddles, increasing shareholder value, or company market share, or worker productivity, just doesn't jazz the average worker. Grasp that concept. There is often a huge disconnect between what is important to a company's executive body and what is important to front-line workers. What matters to the average worker are career opportunity, meaningful work, a balanced life, a fair wage, and being treated with respect. Not increasing output. As a middle manager, you have to attend to the goals of your bosses *and* to the career aspirations of your workers. Too many managers focus solely on the former.

It only takes four words to understand the career aspirations of your workers. But they are among the most important words in the English language. Together they constitute what I call the *Holy Question*: **What do you want?** Answering those words, in my opinion, should be required of every job candidate, every worker, and every executive on up the line. The answer to those words should be reviewed during every performance appraisal, succession-planning session, and employee-ranking process. Why? Because when you know what people want, you are in a far better position to match their aspirations to the company's goals. When company and worker goals are aligned, people pursue organizational goals with the same dedication and passion as they do when driven by self-interest.

How does this relate to modulating comfort? It has to do with goals. It's easier to get people to perform courageous (and uncomfortable) tasks when those tasks tie in to the attainment of their personal goals. By knowing what people want to get out of work, you can give them stretch assignments that connect project tasks to their own goals. So if your boss's goal is to "repurpose our existing product assets to create new revenue streams and optimize our market dominance on a go-forward basis," you can tie your boss's goal to your employee's own career aspirations by saying, "Hey John, you said that you want more opportunities to use your creativity. Create ten new business uses for this product by next week."

The point is this: Before getting workers to carry out uncomfortable tasks in pursuit of the company's goals, you have to understand what is important to them individually. Getting each person to answer the Holy Question, with specificity, will help you to know the goals for which they are willing to be courageous.

Provide Energy-Creating Challenges

Few things generate as much positive energy as a worthwhile challenge. At best, comfort conserves energy. At worst, it shuts it off altogether. But challenge does just the opposite. The greater the challenge (as long as it's truly attainable), the more energy it inspires. When John F. Kennedy set forth the challenge of landing a man on the moon by the end of the

1960s, he explained, "We choose to go to the moon in this de-cade and do the other things, not because they are easy, but because they are hard, because that goal will serve to orga-nize and measure the best of our energies and skills, because that challenge is one that we are willing to accept, one we are unwilling to postpone, and one which we intend to win...."

Executives often talk about the desire to tap into peo-ple's passion. Passionate employees work with more gusto than their dispassionate peers. The interesting thing is that the word *passion* doesn't just mean energetic dedication; it also means having a willingness to *suffer*. The word itself comes from the Latin *passio*, which literally means "to suf-fer" (as in the *Passion* of Christ, seen in *passion plays* dur-ing the Christian holiday of Easter). A world-class pianist, for example, will suffer through years of after-school practice, forgoing the creature comforts enjoyed by her schoolmates, in order to earn the right to play on the world stage. Your job, as a manager, is to provide each of your workers with chal-lenges that they would willingly suffer through in order to attain their own career desires. As Kennedy noted, doing so organizes the best of their energy and skills.

Early on in my career, when I was starting out in the field of organizational development, my goal was to become a consultant. My boss's goal, however, was to grow the con-sulting business. He also wanted to make sure that I knew every aspect of our company's consulting products before letting me consult with clients. Doing so would enable me to offer them a full breadth of consulting solutions beyond my own knowledge, which at the time was limited to what I had learned in graduate school. So he tied his goal (to grow the consulting practice) to my goal (to be a consultant) by challenging me to first spend time in a sales role before becoming a consultant. He knew that the move would challenge my comfort. After all, sales was far afield of my educational background. Asking prospective clients for their business would take the kind of gumption that they don't teach you in graduate school. But my boss also knew that the challenge would tap into my passion. I'd be willing to suffer through all the rejection that comes with a sales job because doing so would help me to acquire skills that would make me a better consultant. My boss knew that consulting, like sales, is about accurately defining clients' needs and then providing solutions that fill them. So instead of dreading the sales role, I was excited by the challenge. I saw it as a chance to sharpen my skills at unearthing clients' true needs, skills that would ultimately benefit me as a consultant.

Practice Lead-Ups

As a manager, you have two primary jobs: leave the company better off than you found it, and leave people better off than you found them. The former is achieved through the latter. Thus you have to keep sight of each person's potential, because in helping them to actualize their potential, you help the company to succeed. Often you'll have a richer understanding of people's potential than they themselves have. The temptation is to push them to the edge of that potential too quickly, giving them challenges that eclipse their preparation. Modulating comfort is a better approach because it al-

» You have two jobs: leave the company better off than you found it, and leave people better off than you found them. You get the former through the latter. »

lows you to give workers incrementally more difficult challenges that groom their skills in a measured way. In the sport of diving we called this process doing our "lead-ups."

Lead-ups are the building blocks of complex assignments, and using them greatly enhances people's level of preparedness. If you bypass all of the little skills that *lead up* to the complex tasks you want your workers to achieve, you lower their chances of being successful. No high diver in his right mind, for example, would jump off a hundred-foot high-dive platform without first doing hundreds of jumps at lower levels. Indeed, the path to becoming a high diver starts by doing endless jumps off the side of the pool deck, about two feet off the water.

To illustrate how lead-ups work, let's say you're managing a team that's responsible for generating data reports for the company's senior executives. Your boss has started to complain that the reports seem like little more than "data dumps," requiring her to interpret too much data herself. Going forward, she tells you, she wants your team to interpret the data and make recommendations for actions that the senior executives should take. In essence, she is asking that your team members stop thinking of themselves as data analysts and start seeing themselves as business consultants.

In this case, the temptation is to expect your team members to instantaneously make the shift from analyst to consultant just because you said so. The reality, however, is that making the transition requires gaining a deeper understanding of the business and its goals. It requires developing strategic-thinking skills and the ability to shift between line-item details and big-picture implications. More challenging, it requires changing each worker's self-concept from a provider of data to a provider of advice. For an advice giver the risk is higher, because if a worker's advice proves faulty after the senior executives have agreed to follow it, the impact to the business is much more consequential than when the worker just provided raw data. Because all of these reasons conspire to make such a transition extremely uncomfortable for employees, the situation is ripe for using a lead-up approach. Modulating comfort in an incremental way makes all the changes associated with the transition more absorbable.

How might lead-ups be used to modulate comfort in the case above? You could start by informing the team about the reasons behind the shift in their roles, tying it to the company's goals *and* to how the new skills will benefit them as professionals. Then you could ask them what excites them about the job shift *and* what concerns they have. Maybe you could then offer them training on strategic thinking, or on major trends impacting the business. Next, you could take an old data report and have them brainstorm recommendations they would have made, had they been business consultants and not data analysts. Then you could have them run a sample report and present recommendations to you for your feedback. Finally, you could have them do what the whole process was *leading up* to: creating the report and recommendations that your boss is looking for. Using lead-ups to modulate comfort helps get workers to do uncomfortable things that in the absence of an incremental approach they might not have done. With each lead-up, the employee is exercising more courage.

After the Courage Foundation Is Built

Jumping first, creating safety nets, harnessing fear, and modulating comfort are management tools for setting a foundation that supports and encourages courageous behavior. Part 2 of the book, chapters 6 through 9, provides stories and examples of what can happen once the foundation is built. These chapters explain, in greater detail, each aspect of the *TRY, TRUST, TELL* framework. Having a way of categorizing courageous behavior allows you to pinpoint the exact type of courage that each individual worker may be most in need of building. Courage *really* goes to work when managers build a strong foundation of courage and then provide courage-building assignments that are specific to the individual needs of each worker.

Questions for Reflection

In what ways are your workers too comfortable? In what ways do they play it too safe?

_____

_____

_____

How would *you* answer the Holy Question? *(What do you want?)* How would your boss answer it? Your customer? Each of your direct reports?

_____

_____

_____

What work challenges would simultaneously tap into each worker's passion *and* serve the goals of the business? What lead-ups could be used to make the challenges bearable?

_____

_____

_____

Part II

Three Buckets of Courage

The last four chapters were devoted to putting a foundation in place that supports courageous behavior. Now that the foundation has been set, it is time to shift our attention to the types of courageous behavior that the foundation supports. Understanding (and influencing) courageous behavior requires that you be well versed in the different ways that people behave when their courage is activated. To set up the chapters in part 2 of the book, let's first get reacquainted with the Three Buckets of Courage.

TRY Courage

Progress, in work and life, results from attempting new and uncomfortable things. *TRY* Courage is the courage of first attempts, and you experience it whenever you attempt something for the first time, or reattempt something after a significant failure. Whenever situations require taking hold of opportunities, blazing new trails, or applying hands-on leadership, it is time to fill up the *TRY* Courage bucket. Of the three types of courage, *TRY* Courage is the one most associated with *action*.

Most new work tasks don't come with training wheels. Whenever you attempt something new, such as leading a new project, you run the risk of crashing, visibly and publicly. People are watching. How you perform as the leader of the new project will impact your boss's success, so she is watching. Your success or failure as the project leader will impact your project team, so they are watching, too. If you fail, your reputation, relationships, and promotability may suffer. If you succeed, you become obliged to attempt even more challenging and public tasks in the future. Because of the heightened scrutiny that comes with stepping up to challenges, instead of putting their *TRY* Courage to work, many people opt for preserving the *comfortable of the current*. This is true even when very little *TRY* Courage is needed to face the task. A lot of people, me included, avoided learning Microsoft PowerPoint and Excel as long as possible because they were too timid to go through the awkward and uncomfortable process of learning new skills. Avoiding took less effort and therefore was an easier choice than trying something new.

Learning how to fill the *TRY* Courage bucket (the subject of chapter 7) is a key management skill. Employees with fuller *TRY* buckets are more self-reliant and require less handholding than those with empty buckets. When workers' *TRY* buckets are filled, they become more willing to attempt new tasks and, eventually, capable of assuming leadership roles themselves.

TRUST Courage

As much as you want your employees to become leaders themselves, you also want them to follow you and your directives. To do that, they have to trust you. *TRUST* Courage is an essential part of being a good follower because followership requires trusting, and relying on, the actions of others. When workers have high *TRUST* Courage, they are receptive to your directions, open to your feedback, and mature in how they handle your criticisms. Their *TRUST* Courage is strengthened when you honor them in the same way.

The opposite of trust is distrust, and distrust taken to its furthest extreme results in paranoia. When workers' *TRUST* buckets are empty, they spend too much time and energy worrying about your "secret motives" for assigning them difficult tasks. They don't give you the benefit of the doubt. Instead of just getting on with the work at hand, they spend time trying to read between the lines, even when the only thing between the lines is white space. Low *TRUST* buckets are no small matter, impacting everything from the cohesiveness of your project team to the earnestness with which workers commit to assignments. For you as a manager, pouring courage into employees' *TRUST* buckets (the subject of chapter 8) is the best way to ensure that they will follow your leadership.

TELL Courage

TELL Courage is the courage of voice and involves telling the truth, regardless of how uncomfortable that truth may be for others to hear. Of all the courage types, it is the most rarely used in the workplace, particularly at the lower levels. Managers often struggle to understand why so many workers lack *TELL* Courage. "What is hard about speaking your mind?" they think. Many managers, after all, rise through the ranks because of the dominance of their personalities, often separating themselves as managers by the ease with which they verbally direct the actions of others.

The harsh truth about why so few employees speak their mind assertively is that workers can and do get fired for being too blunt and undiplomatic. Facing this, many opt for a safer approach, withholding their opinions and sugarcoating their words so that they sound more agreeable. Low *TELL* buckets are the primary cause of people pleasing and ass kissing, communication approaches that are both manipulative and dishonest. But as distasteful as they are, using such approaches rarely gets you fired. Sycophants can have long careers.

TELL Courage comes in many forms. An overloaded worker who musters up the courage to ask his teammates for help is demonstrating *TELL* Courage. So too is the embarrassed worker who says he's sorry after dropping the ball and missing a project deadline. *TELL* Courage is also at play in the much rarer case of the worker who speaks up and disagrees with her boss. Having *TELL* Courage means that the words you're thinking in your head are the same ones that are coming out of your mouth.

When employees have enough courage to assert their opinions candidly, or to sell their ideas with tenacity, or even to give you feedback constructively, you become a better manager and they become more confident people. In chapter 9 you'll learn how to fill your workers' *TELL* buckets.

Figure 2 summarizes the Three Buckets of Courage. Courage, as has been explained, is an enormous concept. But if you focus on the behavioral aspects of courage, such as those associated with each bucket, it becomes more grounded, comprehensible, and influenceable. More detailed explana-

TRY	TRUST	TELL
The courage of action and pioneering "first attempts"	The courage of relying on the actions of others	The courage of "voice" and truth telling

Associated with:	**Associated with:**	**Associated with:**
• Having initiative • Leading	• Being receptive and open • Following	• Truth telling • Asserting one's opinions
Requires:	**Requires:**	**Requires:**
• Overcoming inertia	• Letting go of control	• Conviction
Risks:	**Risks:**	**Risks:**
• Your actions may harm others.	• Other people's actions may harm you.	• Exposing your opinions may cause you to be cast out of the group.

Figure 2.   The Three Buckets of Courage

tions and specific approaches for filling the *TRY*, *TRUST*, and *TELL* buckets are provided in chapters 7, 8, and 9. Each chapter uses real-life client examples to bring the three types of courage to life.

In the next chapter, you will learn more about how the buckets work and why it is so important to fill them with the right stuff. You'll also learn about the impact that your own management style has on whether people behave courageously. As you'll see in the next chapter, when it comes to inspiring (or failing to inspire) workplace courage, managers are both *Fillers* and *Spillers*.

Chapter 6

Fillers and *Spillers*

There is no such thing as a "self-made" man. We are made up of thousands of others. Everyone who has ever done a kind deed for us, or spoken one word of encouragement to us, has entered into the make-up of our character and of our thoughts, as well as our success.

George Matthew Adams

If the employees provide the competitive advantage for some companies to be leaders, they are also the source of competitive disadvantage for average or substandard companies . . . employees create just as many problems as they solve.

E. L. Kersten

"Are you kidding me? Do you realize how at-risk you just put us? Why in the hell would you tell that to our client? How much money we make is none of their business, and you just gave them all sorts of leverage that they will now use against us. You can't trust clients with information like that—believe me, they will take advantage of you every time. You've been here too long to keep making such rookie moves."

If I were a cartoonist, I would draw little puffs of smoke steaming out of Susan's ears. I'd draw thin, tightly pursed lips stretched into a frown. I'd draw bifocals perched at the end of Susan's nose, with her casting down her eyes at me like a prudish librarian. I'd then draw a bubble over her head with the words that she wasn't saying but was clearly thinking: "You dumb-ass."

I hated moments like this with Susan, and I had experienced too many of them in the three years I worked for her. The punishment, in the form of her verbal spankings, never seemed to fit the crime. Sure, as an inexperienced manager I lacked savvy when dealing with customers, but I wasn't a neophyte, either. My crime, in this case, was that I had told a client that our company was having its best year ever. I said it as a way of strengthening the client's confidence in our company—and because, frankly, I was proud of it.

After my meeting with the client, I had gone to Susan to relay to her how well the meeting went. When I told her the part about letting the client know how well our company was doing, she blew a gasket. The way she viewed it, the client would now start pressuring us to whittle down our fees. Even though she hadn't attended the meeting and hadn't witnessed the easy relationship I had built with our client, she was convinced that I had screwed things up. My innocent disclosure proved to her, once again, that my judgment couldn't be trusted. No reasoning on my part would convince her otherwise.

It isn't hard for workers to come up with derogatory and divisive labels for bosses like Susan. Early on, my coworkers and I whispered quite a few of them behind her back. Such terms are restrictive, and exclude the complexities of people and personalities. They also exclude the facets of, and capacity for, goodness that each person has. No one, as the derogatory labels insinuate, is entirely bad. As much as Susan could be uptight and condescending, she was also one of the most brilliant executives I ever worked for. Her thinking was crisp and critical. When I went to Susan with challenges and issues, her brilliant thinking would help illuminate a clearer path to resolving them. Her thinking nearly always made my thinking better.

Susan wasn't a jerk; she was just someone whose *TRUST* bucket was filled with the wrong stuff. When a person's bucket is filled with courage, she will respond to challenges with confidence, conviction, and chutzpah. When the bucket is filled with fear, she will respond with apprehension, tentativeness, and anxiety. Like Susan, most people are courageous in one area and lack courage in another. Susan, for example, boldly took on the complex and higher-risk projects that her colleagues avoided. Her *TRY* bucket was filled with courage. So was her *TELL* bucket, as evidenced by how bluntly she stated her opinions, even when expressing them to her bosses. But when it came to issues of trust, because her *TRUST* bucket was filled with fear, her demeanor would change. Her behavioral disposition would shift from confidence to fear. The more fearful she became, the more her fear would spill out over everyone else.

This *or* That

Too often, organizational theorists divide people into either/or categories. They tell you that you're either technically intelligent or emotionally intelligent. You're either a task-oriented manager or a people-oriented manager. You're either an introvert or an extravert. Such narrow either/or distinctions fail to acknowledge the complexity, fullness, and often-contradictory nature of a person. At different times, and under different circumstances, most of us can be accurately described by any of the labels. With clients I exhibit a different level of emotional, people-oriented intelligence than I do in my marriage, for example.

People are not *either* courageous *or* cowardly. They are both. In one situation a person will behave with bravado. The same person, facing a different set of circumstances, will have no spine at all. The person who has no problem speaking up to authority may be the same person who gets slightly nervous when stepping onto an escalator. Given the dynamic nature of human beings, let me be explicit about the managerial dispositions I am going to introduce next: They are *not* either/or labels. Rather, they are sets of actions and behaviors that are reflective of whether people are operating out of courage or fear. I call these two management dispositions *Fillers* and *Spillers.*

What's in *Your* Bucket?

Susan was what I call a *TRUST* Spiller. Her trust issues often caused her to be suspicious of the motives of others. In situations where another person's motive was unclear, she nearly always assumed the worst. *TRUST* Spiller managers like Susan usually aren't born that way. They learn to distrust after getting hurt by trusting. Most *TRUST* Spillers can point to a betrayal (or *perceived* betrayal) as the reason they withhold their trust. In Susan's case, her father died unexpectedly when she was sixteen years old. Susan's mother was nearly incapacitated by the event, and Susan, as a result, had to become "the responsible one," taking care of both her mother and her younger sister. She shared this with me in a candid and disarmed moment over dinner one night. When I asked her what impact her father's death had had on her, she said, "I learned never to rely on someone so much that when they go away you can't take care of yourself. Never get so close to someone that you'll be devastated when they're gone."

Susan's father's death had taught her that closeness, such as the closeness that trust brings to relationships, is dangerous. So anytime she faced a situation that held the potential of deepening the bonds of trust between her and another person, her demeanor became prickly. Distrust was a protection mechanism, like the bristling of a porcupine's quills when it's threatened. When Susan's defensive spikes were up, she was more apt to lash out at people. Because her moods lacked predictability, people would become distrusting of *her*. By being distrustful toward others, she would, in a roundabout way, get distrust in return. It was as if her *TRUST* bucket had become so full of fear that it would spill over into others' buckets, too.

We behave according to what our *TRY, TRUST*, and *TELL* buckets are filled with. When your bucket is filled with courage, you meet the world with confidence. When your bucket is filled with fear, you see the world (and the people in it) as a threat. Because it is uncommon to have all three buckets filled with courage, most managers are both *Fillers* and *Spillers*.

Putting the Buckets to Work

Good bucket management is a function of three things: 1. knowing which bucket you're operating out of, 2. discerning which bucket your employees are operating out of, and 3. filling your bucket and their buckets with courage.

In a moment I'll share with you the unique behaviors that *Filler* and *Spiller* managers exhibit in each of the respective *TRY*, *TRUST*, and *TELL* buckets. But first it is useful to understand the general *Filler* and *Spiller* behaviors that are common to all three buckets.

As depicted in Figure 3, when your behaviors are directed by a bucket full of courage, you will manage people differently than when your bucket is full of fear. You are a *Filler* manager when you build up people's confidence by encouraging them to face challenges, as you have, in that bucket. You *fill* their bucket with the same courage that is sloshing over in your own bucket. Because your bucket is full of courage, and because you've experienced success within that bucket, you start with the assumption that workers can be successful in that bucket, too. Your own successes are proof that their successes are possible. As a *Filler* manager, you emphasize the gains that people will make by taking risks and building up their courage in that bucket. You are a *Filler* manager when your optimism about the future leaves people feeling more confident about themselves and more energized to deal with whatever challenges they are facing.

You can't encourage people if you are coming from a place of fear. You are a *Spiller* manager when you undermine people's confidence by placing undue emphasis on all the ways they will likely get harmed, as you have been, if they confront challenges in that bucket. As a *Spiller,* you drain whatever courage people have in their bucket and fill it up with the fear that is spilling over from your own. You have experienced failure and pain within that bucket, and you assume that workers will, too, if they move forward. To prevent

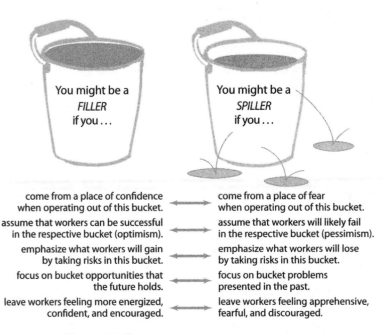

You might be a FILLER if you…		You might be a SPILLER if you…
come from a place of confidence when operating out of this bucket.	⟷	come from a place of fear when operating out of this bucket.
assume that workers can be successful in the respective bucket (optimism).	⟷	assume that workers will likely fail in the respective bucket (pessimism).
emphasize what workers will gain by taking risks in this bucket.	⟷	emphasize what workers will lose by taking risks in this bucket.
focus on bucket opportunities that the future holds.	⟷	focus on bucket problems presented in the past.
leave workers feeling more energized, confident, and encouraged.	⟷	leave workers feeling apprehensive, fearful, and discouraged.

Figure 3.   Fillers and Spillers

them from getting hurt, or to hold them back from gaining successes that you haven't experienced, you discourage them from taking any risks in the bucket. Your focus is on the losses they will incur. You are a *Spiller* manager when your pessimism leaves people feeling discouraged and less confident about themselves and the future.

The most pronounced differences between managers who are *Fillers* and those who are *Spillers* are these: A *Filler* manager assumes the best in people, encourages risk taking and mistake making, views the future with optimism, and makes people feel more confident and courageous. *Spiller* managers do the opposite.

Bucket-Specific *Fillers* and *Spillers*

Rarely is a manager uniformly a Filler or a Spiller. More likely he or she is a Filler in one or two buckets and a Spiller in another. While the Filler/Spiller behaviors just mentioned are common to all three buckets, there are also behaviors that

TRY Fillers *and* Spillers

TRY Fillers

When a manager's *TRY* bucket is full of courage, she will encourage workers to take chances with tangible things, like tasks and projects. *TRY* Fillers value initiative and action. They see facing challenges as the best way to grow and develop; thus they are likely to assign new tasks to workers as a way to help them step up to a higher skill level or standard. They value and encourage novel approaches and experimentation. *TRY* Fillers want workers to make some mistakes, because mistakes are the best evidence that workers are extending themselves.

TRY Spillers

Managers with *TRY* buckets that are full of fear will resist workers' attempts to use different methods and approaches. Yep, these are the folks who hang on to the safe but low-aim words, "If it ain't broke, don't fix it." Sameness, consistency, and predictability are what matter most. Experimentation is viewed as folly or danger. Mistakes are just proof of people's incompetence. "Why go through the effort of extending yourself?" they think. "You'll save energy by doing it the way it's always been done."

are bucket specific. The TRUST Spiller behavior of doubting your intentions, for example, is very different from the TELL Spiller behavior of stifling your opinion. Thus, to make the best use of the Filler/Spiller concept, you have to take into account the specific behaviors that are unique to each bucket.

TRUST Fillers *and* Spillers

TRUST Fillers

Managers with *TRUST* buckets that are full of courage are apt to give people the benefit of the doubt. They start with the assumption that people's actions are based on positive intentions. Rather than making workers prove they can be trusted, they presume that the workers are trustworthy. Thus, delegating work is easier for *TRUST* Filler managers, and they give workers a lot of latitude in how they will get their tasks done. *TRUST* Filler managers encourage people to open up, as they have, in ways that less-trusting people won't.

TRUST Spillers

Managers with *TRUST* buckets that are full of fear guard vigilantly against being taken advantage of. They won't let people burn them like they've gotten burned in the past. Thus, *TRUST* Spiller managers endlessly make people prove they can be trusted. *TRUST* Spillers start with the assumption that people's actions are based on selfish motives and/or bad intentions. *TRUST* Spillers have a hard time delegating tasks. They fear that workers will screw up and make them look bad. *TRUST* Spiller managers lord over workers until the job is completed exactly as the managers would have done it themselves. *TRUST* Spillers have been harmed by trusting people in the past, so to prevent getting harmed again, they put up defensive walls, which makes them closed and/or cold people.

TELL Fillers *and* Spillers

TELL Fillers

Managers with *TELL* buckets that are full of courage have no problem "telling it like it is," and they want workers to do so, too. They value honesty above all else and can be impatient with people who couch their words in vague terms. *TELL* Filler managers encourage people to speak up and get their thoughts and ideas out in the open, like *Filler* managers do, even if those ideas run counter to their own. *TELL* Filler managers stress the importance of showcasing one's ideas persuasively, and view persuasion skills as an essential ingredient for business success.

TELL Spillers

Managers with fear-saturated *TELL* buckets want workers to package the truth in words that are pleasing to the ear but not always honest. "When the boss says something," they'll say, "just agree." *TELL* Spiller managers go to great lengths to avoid being "in trouble" with their own bosses, which makes them consummate conflict avoiders. This makes it difficult to know where *TELL* Spiller managers really stand on issues. *TELL* Spillers discourage people from stating opinions that run counter to the group's, because doing so might cause disharmony.

This *and* That Works, Too

I want to reemphasize that it is rare to have all three buckets filled to the brim with courage. More commonly, a manager is both a *Filler* and a *Spiller*. I recall watching an interview between Donny Deutsch, host of my favorite business television show, CNBC's *The Big Idea*, and Donald Trump Jr. (Donald Trump's eldest son). When asked what lessons he had learned from his father when growing up, Donald commented that as a little boy, when he would be leaving for school, the elder Trump would say, "Remember, *never trust anyone*, not even me." Then, a few moments later, Trump would ask the child,

"Do you trust me?" His son would say something to the effect of, "Of course, I do. You're my dad." To which Trump would feign exasperation and say, "No! I just told you, never trust anyone!"

My hunch is that papa Trump is a *TRUST* Spiller. Certainly anyone who adopts a "Never trust anyone" philosophy fits the mold. Yet who would accuse Donald Trump of lacking courage? His facility for trust is only one dimension, and one measure, of the man. His *TRY* bucket, as evidenced by the bold deals he has made over the years, is full of courage. So, too, as evidenced by his big mouth and willingness to confront just about anyone, is his *TELL* bucket. The point is, it is common for managers to have buckets with both courage and fear. Still, despite the rarity of occurrence, if your aim is to help your workers to be courageous in every facet of their careers while also actualizing your own potential as a courageous human being, filling all three of your buckets with courage is a worthwhile ideal.

Fill 'Er Up!

Courage goes to work most potently when all the buckets are full of courage. Your job, as a manager, is to figure out which buckets—your own and your workers'—are most in need of filling, and then to provide the work experiences that fill them with courage.

As a manager, you're either filling your workers' courage buckets or you're draining them. Many of the ideas you've already read about in the book thus far, such as those associated with the Courage Foundation Model in part 1, are in essence about helping you to fill people's buckets with courage.

The chapters that follow build upon those foundational ideas by offering specific guidance about how to fill each of the *TRY, TRUST,* and *TELL* buckets with courage . . . however, below are some general courage-filling strategies you can apply across all three buckets.

Courage Fillers

Work with the Bucket *THEY* Want to Fill: Often, a manager will ignore a worker's own aspirations to fill a specific bucket. An example of this is when a manager keeps a worker chained to a set of tasks that the worker has outgrown. The manager purposely holds the worker back from learning new skills, rationalizing that he "can't afford to have you working on other tasks right now." Except that "right now" goes on for years, and the manager stunts the worker's growth. A better approach is to identify what new skills and tasks the worker is interested in learning, and provide him with stretch experiences that will enlarge his capabilities.

Use the Fears of Your Past to Build Futures of Courage for Your Workers: While your bucket may be full of courage today, there was probably a point in time when it was full of fear. Plus, while your bucket may now be full of courage, your worker's may be full of fear. Think back to all the experiences you went through, and guidance you received, that helped you to empty your bucket of fear and fill it with courage. Share those experiences with your employee so that he can see his current bucket circumstances as temporary and part of a courage progression.

Teach Workers to Apply *Bucket Borrowing*: As noted, most people have at least one full courage bucket. Bucket Borrowing involves helping a person to borrow the courage she has in one bucket to use in another. A go-getter worker, for example, who has no fear about taking on new projects (*TRY* Courage) can fill her fearful *TRUST* bucket by using the same approaches that she uses with her *TRY* Courage. For example, when taking on a new project, she would likely start with a goal, break down the goal into smaller objectives, and then figure out the actions that would cause the goal and objectives to be attained. You can help the worker to fill her *TRUST* bucket with courage by having her set trust-building goals, objectives, and actions just as she does when setting goals on projects where she applies her *TRY* Courage.

Fill Workers' Buckets to the Right Level: Many managers make the mistake of trying to pour a hundred gallons of courage into a ten-gallon bucket. Instead of underusing a worker's bucket, the manager attempts to fill it beyond its capacity by overloading the worker with challenges that he isn't prepared to meet. The end result is a worker who gets burned out or disheartened because he can't keep up with the manager's demands. This mistake may stem from the fact that many managers judge the size of their workers' buckets by the size of their own. A more effective approach is to pour courage into workers' buckets at an absorbable rate, such as using the *lead-up* approach described in chapter 5.

I'm betting that you're the kind of person who wants to do an even better job of being a *Filler* manager. In each of the next three chapters, you'll be provided with specific tips and techniques that you can use to build workers' courage in each of the respective *TRY*, *TRUST*, and *TELL* buckets. Each chapter uses real-life client situations to illustrate what happens when courage goes to work.

Chapter 7

TRY Courage

Inaction breeds doubt and fear. Action breeds confidence
and courage. If you want to conquer fear,
do not sit home and think about it. Go out and get busy.

Dale Carnegie

The most recognizable form of courage, *TRY* Courage is the
courage of first attempts—trying something for the very first
time. Think back, for example, to your first day of school, or
your first kiss, or the first time you drove a car. At the time,
these firsts were, for you, pioneering events, thresholds that
you had to cross over to ensure your advancement as a member of the human community. While such firsts look ordinary now, when you were actually contending with them, you
were probably desperately nervous.

Managers contend with "trying firsts" all the time. Remember, for example, when you first moved into a management role? Or when you first became responsible for the

performance of an employee? Or when your boss asked you to lead a pioneering initiative for your division? All of those things required *TRY* Courage on your part. Similarly, your direct reports contend with trying situations when they struggle to learn a new and more sophisticated software system, or uproot their families and relocate to a different geographic area, or become responsible for a project of their own for the first time. Such situations are ripe for the development of *TRY* Courage.

Having *TRY* Courage requires overcoming the inertia of the moment. Challenges of initiative heighten a person's awareness of the gap between where she is and where she wants to be. The greater the gap, the more energy, discomfort, and *TRY* Courage will be required to close it. For this reason, a lot of people avoid *trying* because closing the gap just takes too much effort. Unless a person actively deals with the DNA-level inertia that seems to want to keep everything the same, he won't fully experience his *TRY* Courage capabilities. Whether the challenge requires the person to start something new or to stop something he has grown comfortable with, overcoming inertia is key to building *TRY* Courage.

All forms of courage involve taking risks. With *TRY* Courage, the underlying risk is that your actions end up inflicting harm on others or yourself. Who loses, for example, if that pioneering initiative you're leading is a colossal failure? Your people lose, your company loses, and you lose. Such consequences raise the stakes, bringing risk to the situation. Without the risk, however, such situations wouldn't be worthy of your courage.

Because they involve people or organizations attempt-

»
All forms of courage involve taking risks. Risk taking is the application of courage, or courage in action.
»

ing new, pioneering, and risk-infused things, the stories included in this chapter all deal with *TRY* Courage. As with the stories to come in chapters 8 and 9, some of the stories you'll read about next involve the courageous actions of organizations, and some involve courageous individuals. Whether the courage is individual or organizational, all the stories provide instructive lessons about how to fill people's buckets so that courage can go to work.

This first story shows how the TRY *Courage of company leaders can set a powerful example about the type of courageous behavior that is desired of the rest of the organization. The growth and sustainability of organizations, as with individual people, require attempting new things by putting the old and established things on the line.*

Power Play

The Aldridge Electric Company is a large electrical contractor located in Chicago. These are the folks who do true hands-on work, like drilling through layers of concrete, laying thousands of miles of heavy copper wire, and taming a current so deadly that one jolt would fry you crispier than overdone bacon.

Aldridge isn't your neighborhood electrician (though it started out that way). This is the company that installed the lights at Soldier Field so that you can watch the Chicago Bears maul the Green Bay Packers. These are the folks who illuminate the runways at O'Hare Airport so that the jumbo jet you travel on can land safely. These are the folks who keep Chicago safely and perpetually wired. They wire Illinois highways. They wire Chicago's famed elevated railway, the "EL." They wire Chicago's magnificent skyscrapers.

Built on a foundation of *TRY* Courage, Aldridge Electric is a classic American success story. The company was founded by Leonard Aldridge, an enterprising Nebraskan who, before moving to Chicago, drove through America's heartland in his Model T truck picking up small electrical jobs. Since the late 1970s, the company's entrepreneurial legacy has been carried on by Ken Aldridge, who became the company's CEO upon the death of his father.

As much as any company Giant Leap has ever worked with, Aldridge gets it when it comes to courage. Aldridge has earned a reputation as a company that takes on the tough and risky projects that other companies avoid. What Aldridge gets is that courage isn't about recklessness. Aldridge takes on the tough stuff because it creates tightly woven safety nets in the form of rigorous safety standards that often eclipse those specified by the highly regulated projects they deliver. It adheres to a detailed approach to project management and has made a significant investment in training its project managers on up-to-date industry standards and practices. Aldridge is also committed to developing the leadership skills of its managers, and it hired Giant Leap to design and deliver a multiyear leadership program for all of its leaders.

Aldridge also gets that there is a huge difference between ensuring the safety of the workforce and playing it safe as a business, and that the best way to ensure the growth and development of the company is to deliberately Jump First. Aldridge has developed a track record of entering new markets, knowing full well that for a time the company will be at the mercy of a steep learning curve. Aldridge knows that the offspring of *TRY* Courage is experience, and experience is what attracts customers. It was this *TRY* Courage that helped Aldridge muscle its way into Chicago's transit market, eventually winning multimillion-dollar contracts in the process. Transit now makes up a significant portion of Aldridge's business. It was *TRY* Courage that Aldridge relied on when it entered the booming communications market in the 1990s. And it is again *TRY* Courage that is fueling Aldridge's latest new market.

TRY Courage Involves Exploration

TRY Courage involves accepting challenges that you have never faced before. For companies, few firsts are as risky and consequential as entering a new market. A new market entry can have a dramatic impact on the entire business. For one, it requires a significant financial investment. When you enter a new market, there are incumbents who have an established and entrenched reputation among the market's customers. So gaining entry into the market requires a lot of advertising and business-development dollars. Beyond money, entering a new market requires establishing a whole new network of professional relationships. You've got to learn the players so that you can know the playing field. Finally, entering new markets requires training employees in the skills, practices, and standards that are unique to the market. Each layer of commitment (financial, relationship, training) deepens your entry (and investment) into the market. Still, there are no guarantees that you'll be able to outshine the competition and establish a market presence. So the risks of new market entry are very high, which makes such ventures ripe for *TRY* Courage.

Chicagoland is construction land. As the saying goes, Chicago has two seasons: winter and construction. Contractors follow the dollars, and when new money is appropriated by the state or government, companies that win contracts can do quite well. Aldridge's transit division grew when the company won work as part of a massive government highway-spending bill. Appropriations like this come in waves; and in between waves (that is, in troughs), when the government money for projects dries up, construction companies often shrink (by laying off workers) to account for the loss in demand. The leaders of Aldridge Electric, facing a construction trough, made a more difficult and courageous choice: They decided to *expand* the company's capabilities by entering a new market.

America is going green, and as it does, money is shifting to businesses that support renewable sources of energy. Knowing this, Aldridge Electric, the rough-and-tumble electrical construction company from Chicago, decided it was time to become a wind farmer. While wind power currently accounts for only .25 percent of U.S. power output, it is expected to rise to 6 percent by 2020. Companies that are willing to Jump First can, potentially, reap the benefits of growing with the market. Though unconventional, wind farms, with their large electrical turbines, are all about electricity, so it's a logical business play for Aldridge. But jumping into this new market is a risk, requiring much *TRY* Courage. For starters, wind farms are an emerging, and therefore unproved, market. There is no guarantee that they will grow as predicted. Also, there are no wind farms being built in Chicago. Aldridge employees working on wind farm projects will have to travel out of town. While Aldridge has done a substantial amount of work outside of Illinois (for example, wiring the Chesapeake Bay Bridge), most have been one-off projects. Wind farms will require a greater number of employees who are permanently "portable." Quite a challenging proposition for workers with families in Chicago. Finally, moving into wind farms means a significant investment in business development by spending money on such things as traveling to other states to scout locations, purchasing new equipment, and training employees on the ins and outs of a new industry.

For Aldridge, becoming a wind farmer, because it is so risky, has taken *TRY* Courage. And so far the risk is paying off. Within one month of entering the market, Aldridge landed its first wind farm contract—a multimillion-dollar deal. A few months later, it landed another of a similar scale. Through *TRY* Courage, Aldridge was able to rapidly respond to changing market demands and build a profitable new division.

By developing a strong track record of *TRY* Courage moves, the leaders of Aldridge Electric have helped distinguish the company from its competitors. Aldridge is known as the company with a larger appetite for taking on tougher and riskier projects. The size of its *TRY* Courage bucket helps it to win business from clients with the toughest challenges. It also attracts talent. Aldridge's ballsy reputation causes prospective employees with a similar disposition to seek out job opportunities with the company.

What actions can you take to fill workers' buckets by drawing on Aldridge's *TRY* Courage lessons in becoming wind farmers? Here are a few:

Jump First to Build Entrepreneurial Spirit: As the founder of every company ever launched knows, you can't *reap* unless you *leap*! Entrepreneurs jump before others do, and the best way to infuse the workforce with an entrepreneurial spirit is for leaders to Jump First. When faced with market realities that would cause many companies to lay off workers, Aldridge's leadership made the courageous decision to create its own market reality by expanding into a new market. If your aim is to fill your workers' buckets with courage, start by being courageous yourself.

Teach Workers the Dangers of Inaction and Playing It Too Safe: Growth, in business and in life, comes as a result of *not* playing it safe. For employees, job security is gained from expanding capabilities, gaining new experiences, and attempting new tasks—all of which they won't get if they are constantly playing it safe. In the long run, safety is best secured by taking calculated risks. To fill workers' buckets with courage, make sure when assigning challenging tasks to place as much emphasis on the dangers of *not* taking the risks as on the dangers of doing so. The risks of inaction are very often more perilous than the risks of action.

Create Safety Nets of Expertise: Without safety nets, acts of *TRY* Courage would be reckless. Just as Aldridge's move into wind farms leveraged and extended its expertise in electricity, the new tasks you're asking employees to attempt should be an extension of their current capabilities. It is easier for people to be courageous when they've had at least some experience with the task you want them to try. To be most effective at filling people with courage, try building off of their existing strengths and expertise.

Just as a group of leaders can set a good TRY Courage example by Jumping First, so too can lone individuals. As this next story illustrates, one person's TRY Courage can go a long way toward inspiring courageous behavior among many other people. In this case, by having the initiative to take on a tough and politically sensitive challenge, one person was able to enlist two very different organizations to make some courageous moves of their own.

Going Native

When people describe others as being "courageous," most often they are talking about people who step up to a challenge. People who show initiative and act when others fail to. Or people who turn problems into opportunities. In other words, people who demonstrate leadership. *TRY* Courage fuels leadership and is exemplified through the bold and direct actions that leaders take. People like Randy Willis.

Randy is a senior executive with Accenture, one of the world's largest consulting firms. Randy has been around long enough to know that the best place to apply leadership (and to demonstrate *TRY* Courage) is to look for the things that people are complaining about and then do something to remove the complaints. The richest business opportunities are those that satisfy clients' unmet needs.

As a senior executive in Accenture's government practice, Randy knew that state and federal contracts frequently prevent suppliers of government services from

» **The best way to find places to apply *TRY* Courage is to look for things that people are complaining about and then take actions to remove the complaints.** »

using offshore call centers, often citing government security issues as the reason. More often the real reason is because offshore outsourcing is such a political lightning rod that most politicians won't support projects that would benefit from the use of offshore resources. Their constituents would complain too much about American jobs' moving overseas. Randy also knew that, from a business standpoint, high labor rates make "onshore" call center work unattractive when compared with the inexpensive labor found in foreign countries. Such barriers cause many companies and business executives to avoid government call center contracts altogether. But Randy isn't just another smart business developer searching to create new revenue streams; he is a Sioux Indian. So he combined a number of disparate factors and wove them together into something rich with potential. By launching a technology center on an American Indian reservation, Accenture could gain access to a population of people who are eager to work and who, because they live in rural areas where the cost of living is low, could be paid lower wages than non-reservation employees living in urban areas. Cost savings would also result from the fact that Indian reservations are not subject to corporate income taxes. Moreover, having a call center on a reservation would be a politically attractive way to win government contracts.

TRY Courage Is about Filling Needs

Randy is one of those executives who understands the importance of giving back to those who have been good to you. Having lived for a time on an Indian reservation himself, Randy knows how desperate life there can be. He also is well aware of the social injustices that Indians have endured throughout American history. So one might assume that underneath Randy's idea of building a technology center on American Indian lands was a more altruistic motive than sheer capitalism. While on some level the assumption may be true, Randy is quick to point out that his idea really came down to meeting client needs. As he told me, "The fact that setting up a technology center on an Indian reservation will help the Indian community is an added benefit. For me the impetus of the idea was finding a way to meet the needs of Accenture's government clients. What they were asking for was high-quality services at competitive rates delivered *on-shore*. Setting up the venture on an Indian reservation is the best way to meet that need."

People are attracted to ideas that are compelling and courageous. Not surprisingly, the idea met with strong support when Randy introduced it to his Accenture colleagues. The merits of this idea are self-evident; it just made good business sense. The demand for outsourcing is tremendous, and setting up a technology center on American Indian lands would provide Accenture and its clients with an attractive and cost-effective alternative to foreign-run call centers (such as those that Accenture runs in India and the Philippines). Plus, this particular reservation was, in Randy's words, "sticky." He explains, "Unlike most reservations, the Umatilla reservation was carved out of land in rural Oregon and Washington that the Indians had lived on for many generations. The Umatilla reservation is the native land of the Cayuse, Umatilla, and Walla Walla peoples, so the roots run very deep. Setting up the center on another reservation with Indians who bore no connection to the land would likely result in higher turnover.

There is a stickiness to this reservation—people don't like to leave because it is the land of their heritage."

For Randy, the real moment of *TRY* Courage came when he approached the Umatilla tribal board with the idea. Randy had already done a year's worth of research and preparation, reviewing demographic data that pinpointed the Umatilla reservation as being the most desirable. He had also shaped the idea with his Accenture colleagues and created a carefully laid out business case. Such actions not only filled his own bucket with more courage, but filled the buckets of those around him too. Still, there was no guarantee that the tribal leaders would support the idea. Like many reservations, the Umatilla reservation is benefiting from the revenues that its casino brings in. While gaming has come with the usual problems that surround gambling (gambling addictions, petty crime, and so on), it has, for the most part, bettered the lives of the Indian people. The tribal leaders might think, "What need do we have for a new technology company when our financial needs are being met by our gaming business?"

Randy knew the answer: jobs. His plans called for the venture to scale up 350 call center workers and software developers during the operation's first couple of years. If successful, it could scale even larger, perhaps resulting in more call centers. To allay the fears that the tribal leaders would have about investing in the new venture, and to fill them with enough courage to give the venture the go-ahead, Randy would highlight these facts when pitching the idea to them.

As will be discussed in the next chapter, the *TRY* Courage of one person often results in many people having to demonstrate *TRUST* Courage. Randy, as leaders should, had a clear vision of an attractive future. But leaders don't implement visions themselves; they enlist others to share the dream. The venture could succeed only with the full commitment of the Umatilla people, regardless of how much management support and guidance Accenture provided. Creating the idea, as Randy did, involved *TRY* Courage. And for the Umatilla leaders to support and implement the idea, with the knowledge that if the idea failed, their own people would be harmed, involved *TRUST* Courage. But let's remember, in both instances the operative word is *courage*, and Indians, the original pioneers of North America, are a courageous people. The tribal leaders unanimously supported the idea.

Cayuse Technologies is a first-of-its-kind provider of technology and call center services, and is a solely owned enterprise of the Confederated Tribes of the Umatilla Indian Reservation (CTUIR). Cayuse recently opened a state-of-the-art technology facility on the reservation, directly across from the Wild Horse Resort & Casino. Now that it is operational, the facility provides call center, documentation preparation, and software development services. As it is a solely owned business of the tribe, *all* the revenues stay on the reservation. Accenture benefits by having ready access to low-cost technology labor to meet the outsourcing needs of its clients. Plus, it is paid to manage the operations. Cayuse has contracted with Randy and Accenture to manage and staff the facility, as well as to provide the initial training, equipment, and marketing for the venture. In effect, by assuming the management function, Accenture acts as Cayuse's safety net.

The work is at once groundbreaking, opportunistic, and courageous. If the venture proves successful, the idea could spread to other reservations, becoming a viable economic alternative to gambling casinos. It is also conceivable that the idea could result in a "re-shoring" of America—bringing back many of the technology jobs that U.S. companies shipped over to foreign countries to drive down operating costs. Finally, American Indian call centers could provide relief to U.S. customers who have grown frustrated with every attempt to change a flight, question a credit card bill, or resuscitate their laptops only to get someone purportedly named "Bob" on the other end of the line. When talking to call center representatives, Americans, like people in most other countries, find it easier to speak to people who reside within their own country. And what could be more American than speaking to a Native American?

Courage Doesn't Equate with Success

Nobel laureate T. S. Eliot once said, "Only those who risk going too far can possibly know how far one can go." There are real risks associated with launching this new venture. For one, finding skilled technology labor on the reservation hasn't been without its challenges. Also, the cultures of Accenture and the American Indians are dramatically different and could, eventually, clash. Finally, the venture is an *experiment*, and experiments do fail. Applying *TRY* Courage does not guarantee a successful outcome. However, *not* applying *TRY* Courage does guarantee an unsuccessful outcome. If you don't try, how can you succeed? It is through *attempting* (that is, trying), often relentlessly, persistently, and awkwardly, that courage is most exemplified.

Courage precedes success. While courage will influence the likelihood of the venture's being successful, whether or not the venture is ultimately successful isn't what will determine whether all the people involved acted courageously. They are already courageous because they are attempting something hard, worthwhile, and audacious. Even if the venture fails, the people involved in the grand experiment deserve credit for being courageous.

» Courage precedes success. You can fail and still be courageous. Courage is about facing fear and discomfort, not successful outcomes. However, you'll be more likely to have a successful outcome if you're behaving with courage. »

Randy's explanation of his experience with Cayuse Technologies is instructive and provides an apt description of the hallmarks of *TRY* Courage: "A lot of people think of business as solving problems or offering solutions. But business can be about more than that. It can be, and should be, about creating opportunities for people, companies, and communities. If I've done anything courageous here, I guess it's that I'm taking a shot at satisfying the interests of multiple people around a lightning-charged issue [offshore outsourcing] that most businesspeople would prefer to walk away from."

Lessons from Randy's *TRY* Courage

Randy's story shows that one person's powerful and courageous idea is often the most potent influencer of courageous behavior among communities of people. Here are some practical tips for drawing on Randy's story to help fill people's *TRY* Courage buckets in your organization:

Move Workers Counter-Herd: *TRY* Courage often involves watching where the herd is heading (usually away from a problem) and then going in the exact opposite direction (usually toward the problem). In this case, the herd was shying away from government technology work that required offshore call center resources.

Moving counter-herd took courage on Randy's part. *TRY* Courage is most needed at work in areas that are the sources of problems or complaints. Ask your boss or customers what intractable problems they would love to have your workers solve. Directing people to do courageous things in the service of alleviating customers' *points of pain* provides workers with a tangible way of gauging the success of their courageous behavior. Their courage can, potentially, result in happier customers.

Think Opportunity, Not Problem: *TRY* Courage involves a willingness to think independently and optimistically. *Spiller* executives see obstacles as *problems*, and, like Chicken Little, they scurry about, transmitting their sky-is-falling anxiety to the workforce, stressing everyone out in the process. Randy, as a *Filler* executive, saw the obstacles that outsourcing presented as opportunities and devised an integrated, win-win approach to solving them. Rather than run from the politically charged challenge of offshore outsourcing as other executives had, Randy walked straight into it with courage and optimism. His own passion for the idea, along with a carefully laid-out plan for executing it, helped gain the enthusiasm, confidence, and support of those around him.

Draw on Each Person's Uniqueness: Acts of *TRY* Courage are more likely to be successful when they stem from our own unique experiences. Randy's deep knowledge of offshore outsourcing increased the tribal board's comfort with taking the risk. More important, the board members' knowledge that Randy shared their Indian heritage made it easier for them to trust him. The combination of Randy's strong business background and his authentic Indian heritage added to the idea's credibility. Indeed, Randy's background was so well suited to the situation that he may well have been the only person who could have seen the potential in matching the seemingly incongruent needs of Accenture's outsourcing clients with the needs of the American Indian community. When acts of courage stem from people's own experiences, they are more likely to view the acts as important milestones in their own evolution.

Reward Courageous Behavior, Not Just Successful Outcomes

It is important to differentiate between a successful outcome and a courageous act. Being courageous, by definition, means to take on challenges despite the potential for failure. Courageous workers do, in fact, fail. But failure is an outcome and courage is a means. Just because someone fails on the back end doesn't mean he wasn't courageous on the front end. Rewarding courageous behavior is just as important as rewarding a successful outcome.

Organizations shy away from rewarding behavior and attitude because such things are, due to their subjectivity, notoriously difficult to quantify and measure. How do you quantify, for example, whether someone is "positive" or "friendly" at work? Yet who would argue that such characteristics don't matter at work?

Outcomes can be suspect. When an organization structures its reward system exclusively on objective behaviors, just because they are measureable, it often runs the risk of reinforcing the wrong behavior. In such a system, a wretch of an executive, but one who makes big sales, can get away with being a miserable jerk in the office because sales are more quantifiable than jerky behavior.

Just because outcomes are easier to measure doesn't mean that subjective behaviors shouldn't be rewarded, too. As a means to greater organizational performance, courageous behavior will increase the likelihood of better outcomes. A successful outcome, though, shouldn't be required before you confer "courage status" on someone. That would only squelch people's willingness to try. What defines workers as being courageous is taking action despite being afraid or uncomfortable, not whether they attain a successful outcome.

What are the indicators that a person should be rewarded for her courage? Look for these signs:

- Did the person take action on a problem that others had avoided but that the organization wanted solved?

- Was the action a dramatic departure from the person's comfort zone?

- Did the action stretch the person's skills? As a result of being courageous, is the person prepared to take on bigger challenges for the organization going forward?

Trying once is often not enough. When it comes to courage, persistence matters. As the old saying goes, "If at first you don't succeed, try, try again." This next story illustrates the importance of persistent effort—what I call TRY, TRY Courage. Sometimes the most instructive lessons about courage come from the stories of people who fail . . . but who refuse to lose.

Rebound Courage

"Honestly, it was an experience I wouldn't trade for the world. Why? Because this wasn't just a commercial enterprise, this was something that really mattered." The *this* that Lynn Morgan was talking about was the Women's United Soccer Association (WUSA), and it was a spectacular failure.

Lynn was tapped as CEO after the WUSA's first year. She had been providing executive management for two of the league's most successful teams (the Atlanta Beat and the San Diego Spirit) and had caught the attention of the WUSA's board of directors. After a disappointing year under the previous CEO's leadership, the board offered Lynn the position.

The WUSA was an ambitious undertaking, but one that in the late 1990s and early 2000s made sense given the nation's growing interest in women's soccer, inspired by America's Olympic gold medal in 1996 and the record-breaking crowds for the historic U.S. Women's World Cup victory in 1999. These were the years that gave birth to the term *soccer mom*—describing the intrepid suburban mothers who carted around vanloads of kids with dreams of becoming the next Mia Hamm. These were the kids who had watched as Brandi

Chastain, in one of the most memorable moments in sports history, ripped off her jersey straight down to her sports bra, clenching both fists triumphantly during America's stunning World Cup win in 1999—proof positive that women's soccer had come of age.

The WUSA had been launched with seed money from eight investors, each contributing $5 million toward the league's success. The original business plan had projected that the $40 million would sustain the league's eight founding teams for five years. But the projections proved woefully flawed—the league spent all $40 million, and then some, in the first year alone. Lynn's charge in replacing the previous CEO was to turn things around. To that end, she was successful. By the next year, Lynn had cut the losses in half.

"During my first year, it was a dream job," she says. "The league was receiving a lot of positive attention, and I really thought we could turn things around. These were the best women soccer players in the world, being idolized by throngs of young girls across the country and abroad. There was a spirit among us that we were blazing new trails for women in all sports: opening up doors that had previously been closed, allowing these talented young players to truly live their dreams, and instilling hope and opportunities for future players everywhere. Plus, leading the league was personally gratifying. I had the privilege of giving lots of speeches to young women about health and fitness and the role that sports plays in their long-term development and confidence. I even attended a presidential event at the White House honoring women's athletics."

Competitive isn't a strong enough word to describe Lynn Morgan. *Über-competitive* comes closer. Lynn's love of competition was nurtured during her years as a tennis player at the University of Georgia. But Lynn isn't one of those win-at-the-expense-of-your-principles kinds of people. She loves competing for more wholesome reasons. "There's a kind of purity in competing against a worthy opponent. Great sports matches bring out the best in athletes—not just in the physical sense, but in a much more personal way. Competition provides many life lessons about the importance of discipline, preparation, and persistence, how you handle adversity, and ultimately the stuff you are made of."

Were Lynn a less competitive person, the demise of the WUSA might not have stung so badly. While participation in soccer was growing by leaps and bounds, the things that translate into successful business—attendance and television ratings—for the WUSA were low. And while the league wasn't counting on hitting its revenue projections from stadium attendance, this was still an important component driving large advertising sponsorships. The stadium attendance combined with the TV ratings determined how much sponsors were willing to pay for their sponsorships. Soccer viewership, in the States, was so low that securing a good network deal just wasn't possible. Without strong ratings and sponsorship, turning the league around was a no-win proposition.

Lynn tried valiantly to make it work. She reduced the headquarters staff by 40 percent. She negotiated salary concessions (twice) from all the athletes. She requested, and got, salary reductions from general managers. But, in the end, the league and the venture capitalists who were keeping it afloat were losing too much money—over $100 million in three years. As a noble enterprise promoting athletics among women, the WUSA was a winner. But as a financially viable commercial enterprise, it wasn't.

As Lynn describes it, closing down the league was the hardest thing she's ever done. "You don't just flip a switch and turn something like this off. There's a lot of unwinding that you have to do, which prolongs the pain." It would take nearly four months to close out contracts with sponsors, make outplacement arrangements for the administrative staff, and make final payments to all the athletes. As painful as it was, Lynn takes solace in the fact that, rather than declare bankruptcy in order to avoid making good on the league's financial obligations, the board fully funded the shutdown. Everyone got paid what he or she was owed.

TRY, TRY Courage: When Courage Persists

Winners hate losing. For a little while, Lynn internalized the loss of the WUSA. "There were a host of reasons the league failed, but it was easier for people to attribute it to one person: me. So I took a lot of arrows from disappointed athletes and people I had to fire. But that wasn't the hardest part. The hardest part was the feeling that I had personally let down young women everywhere. I can show you letters from little girls who sent me money they had collected at bake sales to keep the league afloat."

Athletes and businesspeople measure things in terms of wins and losses. Lynn hated having to put a check in the *L* column. "It's a strange thing—in the end, the overwhelming feelings of disappointment from that *L* were what gave me the energy to pursue more *W*s. I'm one of those people who work hardest when they have something to prove. Now I was in a position of having to prove myself *to* myself, which was motivating."

Lynn's story highlights a unique variation on the courage of trying—what I call *TRY, TRY* Courage. This is the courage that refuses to give up in the face of setbacks, that persists through suffering.

» **TRY, TRY Courage forges ahead, relentlessly and tenaciously, despite setbacks.**

»

TRY, TRY Courage forges ahead, relentlessly and tenaciously, in the hopes that one's persistence will eventually pay off. And in Lynn's case it has. Since the shutdown of the WUSA, Lynn has led two successful ventures for Manheim, the largest automotive wholesaler in the world (and a division of Cox Enterprises). Under Lynn's leadership, Manheim launched a new high-tech automotive innovation center—called the DRIVE Center—that is now regularly attended by leading automotive companies. Today Lynn is the vice president of Manheim Consulting, a pioneering new company division devoted to providing automakers with leading-edge industry data, analytics, and consulting.

Of all Giant Leap's clients, Lynn is among the most optimistic, creative, and downright inspiring. She personifies what it means to be a courageous worker. For managers who are struggling to fill up people's courage buckets (including their own!), Lynn offers these tips:

Help Workers to Keep "Loss" in Perspective: Remember, there is a huge difference between defeat and loss. A loss today can become the impetus for positive change tomorrow. If you haven't failed at something, you aren't trying enough. Persisting in the face of setbacks is the essence of *TRY, TRY* Courage. Workers, especially competitive ones, can be hard on themselves when things aren't going as planned. A manager's job is to help workers get past momentary speed bumps and continuously bring back their attention to the longer-term aims. In moments where success seems elusive, emphasize the importance of *persistence* as a hallmark of courage. You fill workers with courage when you help them keep loss and failure in perspective.

Give Them Something to Prove: One of the best ways to fill people with courage is to provide stretch challenges that cause people to prove themselves *to* themselves. Having something to prove supplies motivational energy that can be drawn upon when the going gets tough. Such energy can also spur people on to do courageous things.

Help Them Get Back in the Game—Fast: It is common for people to drop into a deep funk after a setback. If your mind festers too long, your bucket starts getting filled with fear in the form of self-doubt. You start to hesitate when making decisions. Often the best remedy for helping people to recover their confidence after setbacks is to encourage them to "get back on the horse" swiftly, even if they feel as if they are trudging at first. Lynn didn't wallow in her disappointment. Instead, she took on a challenging new job within weeks of the league's demise.

As described in this chapter, courage is found in the *attempt*. Filling people with *TRY* Courage involves helping them to attempt new things, take on messy problems that others avoid, and persist in the face of setbacks. All of these, on some level, involve action and leadership. In the next chapter, you'll learn about a kind of courage exemplified in followership. The next chapter introduces bucket number two: *TRUST* Courage.

Chapter 8

TRUST Courage

*To me, there is no greater act of courage
than being the one who kisses first.*

Janeane Garofolo

The only way to make a man trustworthy is to trust him.

Henry Stimson

The act of trusting often requires letting go of our need to
control outcomes or people, our defense mechanisms, and
our preconceptions about what is "right." For hard-driving
controlling types, such as the coffee-clutching professionals
who make up much of today's workforce, this goes against
the grain of everything they stand for. Trust runs counter to
the take-charge ethos that typifies today's business world. In
many companies, the most valued employees are those who,
when encountering challenging situations, control chaos,
force order, and take decisive action. As the Roman poet Vir-
gil said, "Fortune favors the bold."

TRUST Courage, for managers, is a tricky thing. On the

one hand, you need your employees to trust you so that they follow your direction enthusiastically. On the other hand, you have to monitor their performance, which, if done too closely, often feels distrusting. Plus many managers work in companies layered with systems that are inherently distrustful. It is more difficult to fill workers' *TRUST* buckets if you're an extension of a system that doesn't trust them. "Sure," your workers may say, "I'll trust you . . . just as soon as you get the company to stop random drug testing, monitoring our e-mails, and making us submit time reports."

New managers in particular are challenged with *TRUST* Courage. Consider, for example, how hard it is for new managers to delegate important tasks to employees. In such instances, if the employee screws up, it can reflect on the manager, not the employee. Consequently, many new managers struggle to fully let go of delegated tasks, choosing to hover above direct reports like smothering parents. In so doing, they become *Spillers*, thwarting employee development and keeping themselves mired in tasks that they should have outgrown by this stage in their careers.

Delegation involves *not acting* on the temptation to grab the task back from the employee. The ability to delegate is directly proportional to how much *trust* a manager has in an employee. Trust doesn't come easily for new managers (or immature experienced ones), because it involves intentionally refraining from controlling an outcome (or a person). If the manager doesn't trust that the employee will get the job done, he will grab the task back and do it himself—or worse, he won't even give the task to the employee in the first place. The result is a sort of leadership dependency whereby workers wait to be told what to do, like baby birds waiting to be fed. When this happens, a dangerous *Spill* cycle begins; the leader keeps doing the tasks, which keeps the workers from gaining the skills to do the tasks, which keeps the leader from delegating the tasks, which keeps the leader doing the tasks, et cetera.

» **TRUST Courage involves taking risks on other people and accepting that you might get harmed in the process.** »

Trust is risky. When you trust, you become vulnerable to actions that are beyond your direct control. Your success becomes dependent upon someone else's action. The challenge here is one of reliance; you have to give up direct control and rely on the actions of others. It is this lack of control that makes trust so difficult. Trusting *you* can harm *me*. Because of this risk, it takes courage to place trust in others. It takes *TRUST* Courage, for example, to let employees do their jobs without interference. It takes *TRUST* Courage to accept that, despite their best efforts, employees will make occasional mistakes.

Organizational Trust

Even on a broader scale, at the organizational level, trust is challenging. Because organizations are just as vulnerable (if not more so) to being taken advantage of, they often display the very same distrusting behavior as individuals do. For example, despite well-documented evidence of the benefits of telecommuting, many organizations still prohibit the practice due to lack of trust. After all, what assurances can the organization have that employees will actually be working instead of lounging around in their underwear eating Cap'n Crunch while watching reruns of *Gilligan's Island*?

Organizations are made up of people, and just as some people struggle to trust, so do some organizations. This *reluctance to trust* characterizes companies that practice closed-book management, ef-

» Remember, workers give their companies only as much trust as their companies give them »

fectively keeping the workforce blind to the organization's performance. Organizations follow such practices under the reasoning that employees might use the knowledge of the company's finances to demand better salaries and more perks, which indeed could happen. But closed-book management practices only serve to lower employees' *TRUST* buckets. Employees end up wondering, "What else are you hiding from me?" There is reciprocity at work here; workers give their companies only as much trust as their companies give them.

Sometimes the best way to understand how to fill a bucket with courage is to learn about what drains it. As the following story illustrates, honesty, when delivered ruthlessly, can be just as harmful to trust as dishonesty.

Ruthless Honesty

There are a number of factors that contribute to filling a person's *TRUST* bucket. A history of promises kept, the credibility gained through a proven track record, and a positive reputation are all strong contributors. But among the things that build trust, honesty is premier. You trust people who are honest with you. Mostly. As strange as it may seem, and as this story illustrates, honesty, in toxic doses, can hugely undermine trust.

André was the most arrogant executive I'd ever worked with. Giant Leap was brought in by the company André founded—let's call it OSource—at the request of his HR director to lead a strategic planning session. As part of our Courageous Future services (which include strategic planning), we conduct one-on-one interviews with each of the attending executives—in this case, the twelve executives who made up OSource's senior team.

During the up-front interviews, most executives expressed excitement about conducting their first official planning retreat. OSource was a fast-growing open-source software development company, and the competitive landscape was shifting too quickly to run the business with the same decide-on-the-fly management approach that had characterized the company's early years. Many of the execs commented that the company was overdue for this type of planning session. OSource was living on venture capital and, as is often the case, spending money faster than it was taking it in. The fact that the session was going to be held at a rustic mountain inn made the idea of a planning meeting even more appealing.

But when the interview questions turned to the leadership team, it quickly became apparent that there were low levels of trust between the team and André. This was further validated in an anonymous survey administered prior to the session. André's brilliance, apparently, was eclipsed by his ego. With a mixture of intelligence and verve, André, a native of France, had lived the American dream. He had come to the United States after getting his Ph.D. in computer technology.

After a stint working in Silicon Valley during the dot-com boom and bust, André had been left penniless. He started OSource out of his garage (literally) and had seen it grow to become a reputable player in the open-source movement. All this while he was still in his early thirties.

André was the kind of person who inspired both love and hate in the business world. His followers in the open-source software community loved how he made them feel like David taking on Goliaths such as IBM and Microsoft. In my interview with André, he talked pridefully of his software developers as "rock stars"—calling them "the best and brightest technical minds God ever created." André's opinion was backed up by the fact that the company was successfully siphoning off the Goliaths' customers, to the extent that O-Source was attracting much interest from companies wanting to acquire its elite talent and growing clientele. Indeed, a few years after our strategic planning session, the company was purchased for a reported $500 million.

Although most of his "rock star" developers loved him, the sentiments among André's detractors were more visceral. A national business magazine described him as "brash, vulgar, and insulting." The best illustration of André's arrogance (and vulgarity) is from a story that solidified his near-mythological stature in the open-source software community, a story that became known inside OSource as the "SMD Incident." After reading a customer complaint about OSource's services on an Internet message board, André fired back a reply that if the bellyaching customer didn't like it, he could "Suck My D---."

Some of the executives on André's management team had tired of his behavior and were becoming fearful that his

brazen style would jeopardize the company's chances of being acquired for big dollars. But mostly they had grown distrustful of André. Distrustful of his volatile mood swings and
bludgeoning communication style. One exec commented
that André could "rip you a new one faster than you could
cover your old one."

The first part of the strategic planning session was
standard stuff. Review the competitive landscape, assess O-
Source's current and desired places within that landscape,
and identify company-advancing goals to forge the future.
While the group worked with intensity, the real meat would
come during the second part of the session, which was
devoted to assessing the strengths and weaknesses of the
leadership team itself.

I knew how much the levels of trust on the team needed filling and how dangerous low trust can be for a leadership team, so when I presented the summarized results of
the one-on-one interviews, I was careful to highlight the data
that related directly to trust (or lack thereof). As I did, I could
see André growing visibly annoyed. Finally he reached a boil-
ing point, blurting out, "I am shocked. Shocked! How could
this team have low trust? What's not to trust?! I tell all of you
everything. I am always honest with you, and you know it. If
anything, these results prove that you're not honest with me.
No one had the guts to tell me these things to my face."

The other team members were silent. So I prodded
them. "Listen, prior to our interviews none of you knew me,
but within thirty minutes into the interview you were telling
me things that you're not telling each other or André. Like
I said at the start of the session, the most important guid-
ing principle that we all must follow while we're here is to be

courageous. With that in mind, can anyone help shed light on the trust issue for André?"

Money can be a liberating thing. Scott, OSource's senior vice president of business development, had made enough money in a previous tech venture that he had reached the point where he was working because he wanted to, not because he had to. Plus, he was a seasoned and talented guy. André needed Scott more than Scott needed the job. So the risk of upsetting André was much lower for Scott than it was for the other members of the team. Still, Scott chose his words carefully. "You're right, André, you are honest with us. But a lot of times your honesty is brutal. We live in the South, André, and some people, myself included, get offended by both your 'honesty' and your profanity. The fact that you tell us the truth meets only a minimum standard of professionalism. Try wrapping some courtesy around the truth when you tell it, too—you'll get a much better response out of us."

Scott's willingness to speak up to André caused others to chime in. One person talked about being mortified by the SMD Incident. Another talked about being humiliated when André gave him a verbal dressing-down in front of his direct reports. And another spoke of the opportunity that André was missing to be a positive role model for the rest of the workforce.

To his credit, André was taking it in. Until that moment, André had always prized "intellectual honesty" above all leadership virtues. But he had never considered the impact, emotionally and financially, of extreme honesty. Then I shared with him the story of another CEO, who had written a brutal e-mail to his managers that quickly got posted on a Web site, and how his action wiped out 25 percent of the company's shareholder equity within three days. Like many senior executives, André thinks in *cause and effect* and *dollars and cents* terms. He had no interest in wiping out any of the potential value his company could fetch. Shaping up his behavior was the best way to prevent that from happening.

A few weeks after the planning retreat, I visited with André to see how the plan was taking hold. "Come on, Bill," he said, "let's be honest. Any first-year grad student can lead a strategic planning session. The plan is great and will help us achieve our goals, so you'll get your money. But the real value of the offsite was where it took us as a leadership team and me as a leader. I was absolutely shocked by so many things. I was shocked that I was the only one who thought we had a lot of trust on the team. More shocked that until the retreat no one had confronted me before. And even more shocked that in all my years in business I had never discovered the relationship between honesty and distrust. It is humbling, Bill. I always prided myself on having the guts to say what no one else would. What I couldn't see was that *how* I said those things mattered as much as what I was saying. The truth doesn't mean squat if it isn't delivered with respect."

André's story illustrates some important points about filling up buckets of *TRUST* Courage:

Match Honesty with Courtesy: Honesty, when delivered with brutality, tears trust down. It's a copout to deliver a message with contempt and violence and then justify it by saying, "I was just being honest." People's expectations have evolved past the minimum standards of "just being honest." Honesty doesn't build trust unless it is also delivered with tact and courtesy. Words matter, and when they are used to control, subjugate, punish, or harm, they only serve to obliterate trust, even if the sender was "just being honest." As a manager, you'll build trust more effectively by matching truthfulness with courtesy.

Practice Respectful Management: One of the primary characteristics of emotionally abusive relationships is the use (or *mis*use) of power to control the behavior of others. André communicated obnoxiously because he could. On the surface, such a strategy made him more powerful. But despite his brilliance, André was blind to the negative impact his arrogance was having on his own team. Loyalty produced by fear is, in the long run, unsustainable. As a manager, you'll get deeper levels of loyalty and trust by treating people with respect. Respectful behavior is a great courage filler.

Build *TRUST* Courage from the Get-Go: It's been said that there's no such thing as "instant trust." I disagree. Under the right conditions, trust can be gained surprisingly quickly. Because I am a consultant, people often trust me more in the first few minutes of knowing me than they trust teammates they've worked with for years. Partly this is a function of the *expectation* that comes with my role as an outside, assumedly neutral, party. As a manager, you'll find that clarifying the expectations you have of each team member helps to create a trusting environment. From the get-go, establish the ground rules with regard to keeping confidences, as well as your expectations regarding the professionalism with which workers communicate with one another.

Courage is contagious. As mentioned in the previous chapter, one person's courageous act often spawns whole bunches of courageous acts by other folks. This next story revisits Cayuse Technologies and shows how the TRY Courage of a leader frequently results in TRUST Courage among followers.

Mighty Horses Running

In the last chapter you were introduced to Cayuse Technologies, the company owned by the Confederated Tribes of the Umatilla Indian Reservation. You also learned about Randy

Willis, the Accenture senior executive who, applying *TRY* Courage, birthed the idea of solving a problem for his clients by setting up an onshore call center on tribal lands. As mentioned, the *TRY* Courage of one person—typically a leader—often requires the *TRUST* Courage of others to be successful. With Cayuse Technologies, Randy's vision required a whole lot of trusting from the tribal board and the American Indian employees.

It is fair to say that many American Indian people are distrusting of white people, justifiably so. Their history with the U.S. government is marked by one broken treaty after another. Many tribes were forcibly removed from their native lands and transported to remote places that were barely habitable. During the 1800s, the government aggressively pursued policies to eradicate indigenous languages and cultural practices in order to "civilize" the tribes. On top of that, early contact with white people introduced foreign diseases like smallpox and typhoid fever, killing hundreds of thousands of Native people. It is not an overstatement to say that the U.S. government, and the white men who led it, decimated the American Indian people.

Distrust is a byproduct of betrayal. Given such a stark history, the American Indians' distrust of the white man's way of life makes sense. Although they have long been skilled traders, they have little "corporate" experience beyond gaming. Big business, from the perspective of many in the American Indian community, is too similar to the U.S. government to be trusted without scrutiny. The distrust is magnified by the knowledge that the values and ideals of big business are, at first glance, at odds with the Indian way of life. Indians are about *close-knit community, environmental harmony,* and *personal nobility*. Business is about *maximizing profits, exploiting resources,* and *creating demand* through marketing.

Distrust simmers beneath the surface between people, directing behavior in subtle and even unconscious ways. Harbored resentments, moody behavior, and abrasive communication are all examples of what happens when distrust, consciously or unconsciously, imbues relationships. In business settings, distrust can take many forms, such as uncooperative behavior, passive or active resistance to company directives, or, in the worst instances, sabotaging company goals.

For Cayuse Technologies to be successful, ensuring high levels of trust throughout the enterprise will be critical. Knowing this, Randy contacted me to lead a two-day kickoff meeting with Cayuse employees to create the company's core values. Randy and I had worked together during my years at Accenture, where I had spent six years as an executive in the company's change-management practice. During that time, I had come to admire Randy for his knack for creating business opportunities and his commitment to workforce development. So when he explained his goals for the session and gave me the background on Cayuse Technologies, I knew that it would be something special for Giant Leap to be involved with.

Although Cayuse is solely owned by the Umatilla people, the operation was to be managed by Accenture. Call center management is one of Accenture's core competencies, and its depth of experience in the area would help accelerate Cayuse's entry into the market. But without strong and trustful relationships between Cayuse's mostly Indian workforce and Accenture's mostly non-Indian management, the venture could fail. Success would come down to having *TRUST* Courage between people.

TRUST Courage involves taking risks on other people. It is most often found in situations where the actions of others, despite their good intentions, can harm you. If Cayuse Technologies were to fail, not only would a good number of American Indians be out of work, but it would also be a poor reflection on the reputation of the tribe as a whole. Trusting Cayuse's leadership to make good business decisions would take courage on the part of the workforce. At the same time, trusting the workforce to dedicate themselves to working hard would take courage on the part of leadership. The stakes were high, and each group was at risk.

Deep trust is gained over time. Unfortunately, start-up ventures do not have the benefit of a shared history to help in the creation of strong, trusting bonds the way more mature organizations do. Knowing this, we decided that the core values session needed to be a memorable experience that people could reference as a seminal moment in the company's emerging history. Gaining people's trust would require harnessing their fears. To do that, the session would need to honor the heritage of the Native people and give them a true voice in charting the company's destiny. So, to the delight of the participants, after a few brief words of introduction Randy led the entire workforce out of the Tamástslikt Cultural Institute (where the meeting was held) to a small field where an anthropologist was waiting with two horses. In

»
Building *TRUST* Courage involves releasing control to others, giving them a voice, and sharing vulnerabilities.
»

drawing distinctions between the two horses, a mustang and a Cayuse horse, she created a metaphor that the participants would draw from throughout the meeting. She talked about how the Cayuse horse was small but mighty, how it was fiercely loyal, and how—because of its large chest—it could outlast bigger horses when traveling up steep mountainsides.

People are more apt to trust you when they feel heard. Developing a solid set of core organizational values that people could uphold and honor would require that the values be reflective of their own individual values. So, to start the session, we asked questions that would help us discover what each person's values were. In small groups, they answered questions like these: What drew you to Cayuse Technologies? What are your greatest hopes for the venture? What concerns do you have that need to be addressed? What values would make you so proud to follow that you would stay personally invested when the going got tough? Each question, gently but intentionally, moved them beyond the comfort of preconceptions they might have been holding about American business. We were modulating their comfort by asking questions that influenced them to consider and create new reference points.

The discussions that followed were rich and compelling. One man, a thirty-eight-year-old teacher, spoke of wanting to create a more stable life for his seven children. A middle-aged woman spoke of having just returned to the tribe after the death of her husband and after spending twenty-two years living in Oakland, California. For her, working at Cayuse would allow her to reconnect to life on the reservation while feeding her passion for business. Many spoke of the opportunity being a once-in-a-lifetime chance to better the lives of the people on the reservation.

Having worked with more than a few companies whose core values were nothing more than stale and uninspired words adorning the corporate hallway, we decided that the core values Cayuse would create would need to honor the spirit of the American Indian people while establishing the company as a viable business enterprise. The questions we had asked thus far were all lead-ups to the key question that would help define Cayuse's core values: *On your journey to become a world-class commercial enterprise, what aspects of your heritage do you need to take with you?* Again, the answers were rich. People talked about the need to work harmoniously, as they do on the reservation. They talked about wanting to create a close-knit, family-like environment. And they talked about the desire to be fierce, loyal, and mighty, like the Indians of their heritage.

There was more going on here than creating core values. People, managers and workers alike, were getting vulnerable with each other at a basic human level. This is how *TRUST* Courage is built. Trusting others is much easier when you know their hopes, their dreams, and their fears. Trust also comes more easily when you know what others value, and when those values are compatible with your own. If I don't know you, I may assume the worst in your motives. But after I find out that, like me, you love your children, or that you're taking care of an ailing parent, or that you just lost your husband, I'm much more likely to trust you and see that behind your actions are good and decent intentions. This was not a session about "getting workers on board" or "understanding what leadership has in store for us." This was about people connecting with people through their values. This was

» We are more apt to trust people when we know their hopes, dreams, values, and fears. And they are more apt to trust us when we share those things in kind.

»

about building strong bonds of trust through shared vulner-ability and mutual reliance. This was a session about building *TRUST* Courage between people.

Giant Leap has had the good fortune of working with some of the most respected and admired names in business. We have led sessions in places as diverse as London and Talkeetna, Alaska. Our work as courage builders has been extremely gratifying. Yet, working with the employees of Cayuse Technologies on the Umatilla Indian Reservation in rural Oregon was extra-special, broadening our insights beyond our ordinary scope of awareness. The core values they established reflect all that's good about people and business. Sprinkled throughout the core values of Cayuse Technologies are words that reflect the spirit of the American Indian people—words like *mighty, loyalty, harmony, pride, heritage, heart, community,* and *fiercely committed*.

More meaningful than the words were the images that accompanied them. To solidify the positive memories about the session, we gave each small group a matted canvas, containers of colorful paints, and a bunch of paintbrushes. Each group was asked to create an image that would reflect the spirit of a particular core value and honor the people's heritage. The images were bold and poignant. The core value of quality was shown as a feathered arrow piercing the middle of the sun. Diversity was shown as horses of different colors, prancing according to different temperaments. Teamwork was illustrated by a bald eagle with three Native people dancing above it. The only thing that could soar above the mighty eagle, as was explained, was a strong, unified, and happy team. The pictures* allowed the group to honor the spirit of the meeting in an enduring way and to create visible ideals to which to aspire.

*To view these pictures go to http://www.cayusetechnologies.com/corevalues.html

Here are some steps you can take to fill your workers' buckets with *TRUST* Courage in the same way as Cayuse Technologies has:

Strengthen *TRUST* Courage through Vulnerability: People trust each other when they become willing to be vulnerable with one another. Knowing coworkers' values, hopes, and fears helps you to understand their deepest motivations and intentions. What betrayals, real or perceived, might they have experienced in the past? As a manager, instead of having people "prove" their trustworthiness to you, spend time learning about who they are and what they value. Understand the criteria that each person uses to decide whom they will trust. Ask each person on your team to complete the following statement: *I will trust you when . . .*

***TRUST* First:** Jumping First is important when it comes to trust. It is tempting for you as a manager to want to turn trust into a *quid pro quo:* I will give you trust after you give me trust. Such strategies usually produce a stalemate, with no one person fully trusting any other person. Is it possible that your workers need more trust than you are currently giving them? If so, what is blocking your ability to be the first one to trust? What would it take for you to Jump First and trust first?

(To learn more about Giant Leap Consulting's work with Cayuse Technologies, visit the home page of our Web site and select the case studies [www.giantleapconsulting.com].)

A Final Thought about Trust

Trust is always a risk. But not trusting is far more dangerous. When trust is lacking, distrust fills the void and suspicion reigns supreme. Without trust in ourselves, our dreams languish or die. Without trust in others, we become joyless and isolated people.

TRUST Courage requires assuming the risk of getting harmed by others. It also means growing up and accepting that people are imperfect beings. Some people will hurt you unintentionally, and others, far more rarely, will hurt you with malice. Either way, people *will* hurt you. But the benefits of trusting courageously far outweigh the risks. For it is in trusting ourselves that we validate our own self-worth. And it is in trusting others, or *en*trusting them, that we validate their worth as fellow human beings. Ultimately, *TRUST* Courage satisfies the need that distrust aims to achieve: protection. For in courageously trusting each other, we deepen our relationships and strengthen our communities to the point that the harm that any one member of the community could inflict is made irrelevant.

As discussed in this chapter, *TRUST* Courage involves taking risks on other people. While there are dangers in doing so, there are also deeply enriching rewards. At work, full *TRUST* buckets result in deeper loyalty and commitment. High levels of trust also result in less time being spent dealing with the inefficiencies that typify suspicious work environments. More important, *TRUST* Courage provides you with access to the best qualities that relationships have to offer, like friendship, support, joy, and love.

In the next chapter you'll learn about the third type of courage, *TELL* Courage. It puts words to the first two types of courage, and for some it is the most difficult courage of all.

Chapter 9

TELL Courage

I never did give them hell. I just told the truth,
and they thought it was hell.

Harry S. Truman

Expose your ideas to the dangers of controversy. Speak your mind
and fear less the label of "crackpot" than the stigma of conformity.

Thomas J. Watson

"Your opinion matters to us, really."

"We want your input as we move forward."

"These changes will impact you, so please tell us what you think."

For all the talk about wanting people to be open and honest, the reality is that many organizations stifle (or punish) such behavior. If this weren't the case, surely more people would have spoken up sooner about the breathtaking misdeeds at companies like Enron, WorldCom, Adelphia, Cendant, Dynegy, ImClone, Vivendi Universal, Waste Management, Global Crossing, and Tyco. It's important to remember that most organizations are *not* democracies.

The average employee does not get to vote on which senior management decisions he or she will endorse. As one-party systems, most organizations more closely resemble authoritarian regimes than they do free and open societies. Employees aren't "citizens," and the ability to influence companywide decisions is restricted to those in the upper echelons. So regardless of how open a company considers itself to be, the risks of voicing an opinion that runs counter to the directives of the senior team are so high that most employees keep quiet. In the case of *TELL* Courage, the risk is that in voicing your true opinion, you'll be set aside as an outcast from the established social order. The risk that comes with *TELL* Courage is the risk of social banishment.

Having worked with thousands of employees over the years, I have come to believe that the *TELL* Courage bucket is the one most in need of filling. Employees are quite skilled at biting their tongue. Rather than outwardly disagree with company changes—and risk being viewed as mavericks or outsiders—they "go along to get along." But just because employees actively nod their heads "yes" doesn't mean they aren't passively behaving according to "no." Many company initiatives are dead on arrival because the senior executives misjudged the lack of true commitment to the initiative that lower-level employees had in the first place. They had surface-level yes but commitment-level no.

The lack of *TELL* Courage demonstrated by employees is directly related to the behavior of managers. Specifically, when managers use intimidation to get things done, employees learn that speaking up is the best way to get thrown out.

Intimidation is a powerful behavioral weapon, and when the intimidator has power over you (such as the ability to fire you), it doesn't matter if you're a bodybuilding muscle-head— a weakling boss can still make you shake with fear. Thus, of the three courage buckets, *TELL* Courage is, for a lot of employees, the hardest to fill.

Immature managers may think their job would be easier if people would just "shut up and work." More mature managers know, however, that *TELL* buckets full of fear make their jobs harder. One of the cardinal rules of good management is *No Surprises!* A manager's job is made exponentially more difficult when employees are too afraid to come forward with problems until the problems become too broken to be fixed. Filling workers' *TELL* buckets with courage is the best way of ensuring that workers will overcome the fear that they'll be in trouble if they tell you about problems as they arise.

Fearful *TELL* buckets present real dangers to managers. When employees shut up, managers aren't able to gauge how committed they are to company changes. When employees shut up, managers become closed off from front-line information that could enhance their decision making. When employees shut up, managers lose valuable ideas that could produce revenue-generating or cost-saving innovations. When employees shut up, progress suffers. For this reason, filling employees' *TELL* Courage buckets is one of the most important of all managerial functions.

» *TELL* Courage is the courage of "voice." It involves having independently formed opinions, telling the truth, and being accountable for your own mistakes. »

Confronting company intimidators is particularly challenging for employees. But such challenges also present opportunities to demonstrate TELL Courage. The following story illustrates the difficulties and necessities of TELL Courage. Many times, the most courageous conversations are those that take place one-on-one.

The Ogre on the Runway

Chicago's O'Hare airport vies for the top spot as the world's busiest airport. Twenty-four hours a day, every day of the year, flights from all over the world take off and land at O'Hare. To keep things running safety and smoothly, it is critical that O'Hare's runways are well maintained and well lit. Therefore, O'Hare is continuously modernizing and rehabilitating its runways. But because of the intense volume of air traffic, O'Hare doesn't have the luxury of closing down any runway for an extended period of time. Much of the refurbishing has to happen on the fly, so to speak, mostly occurring between midnight and 6 a.m.

Troy, a project manager I was coaching as part of a leadership development program for one of our Chicago-based clients, was responsible for modernizing two of O'Hare's runways—a pair of the busiest runways in the world. In the construction business, successful projects require tight integration between management and labor. Project managers (PMs) gather the project specs and requirements, plan the timelines, interact with the client executives, and ensure the delivery of materials and equipment. PMs are the project organizers. Supervisors, on the other hand, work with the unions to line up the local labor, deal with the inevitable day-to-day challenges, and provide hands-on oversight over the field personnel. Supervisors are the project implementers. Because PMs mostly work out of the corporate office, and because part of their job is to coordinate the overall project effort, some PMs hold the inaccurate view that the field labor works for them. Conversely, because successfully implementing a project is contingent upon the field personnel, some supervisors hold the inaccurate perception that they alone are responsible for the project. Giant Leap works with four Chicago-based companies, and all of them have one thing in common: occasional friction between PMs and supervisors.

As Troy explained to me, the friction mostly stems from the different ways that PMs and supervisors learn their trades. Many PMs have no direct field experience, joining the executive ranks straight out of college. Many supervisors, on the other hand, never went to college and earned their positions through the school of hard knocks. Construction is a journeyman's business; there is no fast track. Advancement in the field takes years and years of hands-on project work.

On top of the management-and-labor tension is the constant and unrelenting pressure of the project. Huge sums of money are at stake and the deadlines are tight, so there's no room for slippage. All this was ticking in the background when Brad, the lead supervisor, called Troy at home one Friday night halfway through the project. As Troy explained, "Here I was working sixteen-hour days, seven days a week. The body will only let you push so far. So after working twenty-four hours the night before, I went home and jumped in bed by 8 p.m. to get some rest. PMs are on call twenty-four hours a day, so at 10 p.m. I answer the phone when Brad calls. He tells me to get out of bed, go online, and get him a weather report. I'm still half-asleep, so it takes some time for me to get my bearings while I stumble around a bit. Brad gets so pissed off at me for taking longer than he wants that he blows a gasket and starts cussing me out for everything under the sun. Then, just like that, he hangs up!"

Brad, as Troy explained, was a seasoned vet with over twenty years of field experience. He was familiar with every kind of work situation imaginable. Brad had also seen a stream of young project managers waltz in and start attaching their names to successes he was producing. Over the years he had developed a significant degree of contempt for the PMs, particularly those with no field experience. Eventually, Brad resorted to verbally abusing the "PM prima donnas," partly as a way to show them who the real boss was and partly as a way to keep his field personnel entertained. Though respected by the field labor, he was an ogre in the eyes of the PMs.

"I tossed in bed for over an hour, stewing about Brad's tirade," Troy continued. "The more I thought about it, the angrier I got. Who the hell was he to get away with talking to people like that? I guess this is where the *TELL* Courage comes in, because I got out of bed and called Brad. He didn't answer, so I called the general foreman and told him I was coming down to the airport to get a piece of Brad's ass."

It's interesting to wonder what would have happened if Troy had brushed it off and stayed in bed. Certainly that would have been the choice of many other PMs. But letting Brad's behavior slide would only validate for Brad that intimidation—purposely making people afraid of you—is a successful strategy for keeping people under your control. Yes, were it any other PM, Brad's approach would have worked. But Brad underestimated one critical factor: Troy was an ex-

Marine, and Marines are people
who know the value of *TELL* Courage.

> *TELL* Courage culminates
in *High Noon* moments—
verbal showdowns
that can make or break
relationships.

"If there's one thing I learned
in the Marines, it is that if you don't
stick up for yourself, you won't have
the balls to stick up for other people when they need it. I had
to confront Brad as a matter of self-respect—and frankly, so
that he would learn to respect me."

When Troy got to the airport, the crew was working at
the top of the runway. Brad, however, knowing that Troy was
coming, had driven his truck down to the runway's far end.

TELL Courage often culminates in a *High Noon* moment, a verbal showdown, and this was it. As Troy slowly
drove down the long runway, he knew that one way or another, from this conversation on, things would be different
between him and Brad. In the distance, he could see Brad
leaning against his truck with his arms folded and his head
tilted to the side.

"What do *you* want?" Brad asked, clenching his jaw.

"I'm here to tell you that I didn't appreciate your light-
ing into me tonight. All of us are working hard to make this
project successful. We are on the same goddamned team,
Brad! When you told me to go online and look at the weather
reports, what did I do?"

"Hell if I know," Brad said condescendingly. "I wasn't going to sit there waiting for you just to find out. My crew has
too much real work to do."

"No, Brad, I got up, half-asleep, to get a weather report
that you probably could have gotten yourself." He went on,
"Listen to me, Brad, I am not some enemy working against

you. I'm also not some PM rookie oblivious to how things are done in the field. I spent ten years in the field before moving into management. I still spend more time in the field than almost every other PM you know. Brad, do I ever disrespect you like some of the other PMs you've worked with? No, I don't. I value you too much to treat you like I'm better than you."

Brad, unexpressive, looked away from Troy and stared off into the distance.

"Brad," Troy continued, "I need you to hear me. I came down here in the middle of the night to tell you this: I'm here to help you, and I need you to help me. We're on the same team. Don't ever again talk to me the way you did tonight."

There is often a decisive moment after someone asserts *TELL* Courage. In that moment a choice is made: convince yourself that you are right and dig your heels in deeper, or consider the words of courage and accept the invitation to change. What is told through *TELL* Courage is the truth, or at least one person's rendition of it. The choice becomes to accept that person's truth, or to reject it. Troy was, for all intents and purposes, challenging Brad. For Brad to accept Troy's *TELL* Courage would mean that he would have to accept his own culpability, which is exceedingly hard to do. Brad would have to admit he was wrong (which itself takes *TELL* Courage).

Brad sighed deeply. After a moment, he shifted his gaze back to Troy, unfolded his arms, and extended a hand. "You're right, Troy. I'm sorry."

»

Admitting you're wrong and saying you're sorry are forms of TELL Courage.

»

As Troy tells it, "We shook hands and never looked back. That talk at the end of the runway caused something to change in our relationship. Brad knew I respected all the pressure he was under and all the work he was doing. But that day he also learned that I respected myself. I think that gave him confidence in my abilities as a leader. Though it wasn't my goal, by confronting him I earned his respect . . . and I've had it ever since."

Here are a few takeaways about *TELL* Courage from Troy's story:

Clarify the Dangers of Not Telling: While there are risks in confronting people, the bigger risks are often in not doing so. By withholding *TELL* Courage, workers may become *ogre enablers*, making ogres stronger and employees weaker. As a manager, you should clarify with your team when and how to confront obnoxious colleagues and customers. You'll go a long way toward filling their *TELL* Courage buckets by sharing examples about when you have confronted ogres, too.

***TELL* It Privately:** Intimidating people draw power from having an audience. By offering Brad his *TELL* Courage at the end of a long runway, Troy was able to have Brad's full attention while preventing him from playing to the field labor crowd. As a manager, create the expectation that conversations that could potentially embarrass others should be handled privately and one-on-one. Be sure that when you confront workers about embarrassing issues, you do it out of earshot, too.

Set a Standard of Linguistic Precision: To be most effective, *TELL* Courage involves precision. Troy told Brad *exactly* what he found offensive and *exactly* what his expectation was going forward. As a manager, suggest to your workers that before they confront you or other teammates, they should first write down *exactly* what they want to say and *exactly* what they hope to achieve by exercising their *TELL* Courage. Practice and precision pour the fear out and put the courage in.

The next story, while emphasizing TELL *Courage, shows how all three types of courage work together. In this case,* TRY *Courage and* TRUST *Courage allow for and support the full expression of* TELL *Courage. This story also shows how teams of people can go about filling all three buckets at the same time.*

Going There

In 2007, Giant Leap launched a new courage-building program with the Nantahala Outdoor Center (NOC) called the NOC MBA: Management By Adventure. The NOC is located in Murphy, North Carolina, and is one of the world's premier whitewater and adventure facilities. Numerous Olympic kayaking champions have trained there. The MBA program combines the NOC's rich history as a provider of adventure experiences with Giant Leap's courage-building content and techniques. This is not some beat-your-chest executive hoopla in the woods. The learning doesn't come from "roughing it" without toilet paper. To the contrary—executives stay in luxury mountain cabins that would make Daniel Boone blush. They're also treated to organic gourmet meals throughout much of the experience. Rather than teaching through deprivation, we leave in place all the amenities that senior executives have become accustomed to (comfortable accommodations, tasty meals, wireless Internet access, heinie-soothing toilet paper, and so on). Retaining the creature comforts allows the executives to focus on the business at hand: getting courageous with one another. As the program's facilitator, Giant Leap helps the executives to "go there"—with "there" being the politically dicey or interpersonally uncomfortable subjects that they prefer to tiptoe around despite the negative consequences of doing so.

Although the creature comforts remain, the executives aren't pampered. During the program, they do such things as traverse through a high ropes course suspended forty feet in the air, splash through whitewater while rafting down the cold Nantahala River, and actively engage in all of the courage-related content that Giant Leap presents during the multi-day experience. The program follows a deliberate progression from *trying* to *trusting* to *telling*. Participants first challenge their comfort by going through the adventurous and physically demanding parts of the program (*try*). As people actively support one another during the adventure challenges, they begin to let their guard down, developing a fragile sense of shared vulnerability (*trust*). The high degree of trust that develops becomes the foundation for the meat of the program—having healthy, sober, and often uncomfortable discussions (*tell*) about the issues (strategic, tactical, and interpersonal) that are preventing the team from maximizing its potential. The *try* and *trust* parts of the program help create a supportive environment so that the team can have what my company calls Courageous Conversations without the defensiveness or bitterness that such discussions typically provoke.

Over the years, I've facilitated hundreds of team-building events with companies of different sizes and stature. Although there are limits to the effectiveness of experiential team-building programs, done right they can be a powerful

»
Avoiding interpersonal confrontation is a bigger inhibitor to team performance than misaligned goals, lack of planning, or misguided leadership.
»

means of helping teams to confront themselves. While mis-aligned goals, lack of a detailed plan, and misguided leadership can be significant inhibitors of team performance, very often the largest inhibitor is *avoidance.* That is, avoiding the inter-personally touchy subjects that surround the team like sensi-tive land mines.

Getting to TELL

Even strong teams can tend toward avoidance. Such was the case with a marketing consulting company that participated in our Management By Adventure program. To honor the company's privacy, let's call it RadWorks. The company's workforce, composed mostly of top graduates from tier-one schools, prides itself on offering the same level of marketing intelligence and expertise as big consulting companies pro-vide, but without the stiffness and bureaucracy. Unlike most marketing companies, RadWorks doesn't consider itself a "creative ad agency." Such agencies tend to be order takers, taking direction from their clients and then coming back with marketing ideas built around the client's preferences (which are often very different from the preferences of the client's customers). RadWorks, conversely, helps its clients to iden-tify the right marketing strategies, and then coordinates the overall marketing campaign to ensure that the efforts of all the "creatives" are integrated and strategically aligned. Rad-Work's unique and effective approach has helped it to quickly amass an impressive list of Fortune 100 clients.

The company had grown from two full-time employees to eighteen in just five years, and most had come on board in the two years prior to attending the Management By Adventure program. During the one-on-one interviews conducted before the program, it became evident that everyone genuinely enjoyed working at RadWorks. It also became evident that the company was still in its infancy when it came to defining its culture. But gaining cultural maturity was difficult, as RadWorks was winning more and more out-of-town engagements, forcing employees to spend more time away from the office and each other. People were feeling disconnected.

In interviews we asked people to describe any "Pink Elephants" the team might be avoiding that would be useful to address. During the NOC MBA program, we describe Pink Elephants as sensitive subjects that most people are aware of but avoid talking about. Though the answers varied, two subjects became prominent. First was what a few people termed the "Edict Memo." One of the company principals had sent an e-mail telling everyone that they were required to work a minimum of fifty hours a week and were to report to work no later than 9 a.m. The e-mail also specified that during times when the consultants weren't with the clients, they were to be working in the office (versus working remotely or at home). Although the executive sending the memo was consistently identified as the most courageous person in the company, people felt that the tone of the e-mail was patronizing and dictatorial—hence the "Edict" label.

The second Pink Elephant was a growing recognition that the company was starting to reflect the characteristics of the bigger consulting companies. People felt that the company was accepting too many "me too" projects that lacked distinction or uniqueness. Rather than targeting innovative and edgy marketing projects, they were starting to become order takers, accepting inane work that any creative agency

was capable of doing. They were
beginning to play it too safe, even to
the point of failing to push back on
their clients' bland or ill-informed
ideas. RadWorks was becoming
too traditional and, in the process,
weakening its differentiating position in the marketplace.

» Courageous conversations
are designed to help
teams confront and
address—in a sober and
adult way—issues that
are getting in the way of
superior performance. »

The cool thing about the NOC MBA program is that the
data drives the agenda. Companies enter into the program
knowing that the subjects unearthed during the stakeholder
interviews will likely become the fodder for the program's culmination—a series of structured Courageous Conversations
designed to help the team to confront, address, and move beyond the issues that are getting in the way of superior performance. Nothing is off-limits. Because of our role as an outside
neutral party, participants often tell us about meatier issues
than they tell their own internal consultants or the HR reps.

The Courage Lifeline

During the early part of the RadWorks MBA experience, we
taped a long piece of butcher paper to the meeting room wall
and divided it into five columns (representing each year the
company had been in business). Next we drew a line through
the middle of the paper. The top half of the paper would rep-
resent "moments of courage" and the bottom half would rep-
resent "moments that lacked courage." Participants were given
markers and told to identify, using sticky notes, the courageous
and not-so-courageous moments in the company's history.
Each significant moment in its history was placed on the pa-

per, and the farther away from the midline the moment was placed, the more intensely courageous or not so courageous it was. Giant Leap calls this activity the Courage Lifeline, and we typically use it at the start of a session to help draw attention to the important relationship between courage and business. The activity helped tease out the courageous moments that people were proud of at RadWorks. Such events as the founding of the company, winning a huge project over a more famous consulting company, and persuading a client to implement a Rad-Works idea over a tamer idea of its own were all identified as courageous moments. Moments that lacked courage included performing a large project for free in the hopes of winning more work (which they didn't), accepting a large uninspired low-margin project that any creative house could have done, and failing to push back on one client executive's lame idea for fear of upsetting him.

Later that same day, everyone participated in the NOC's high ropes course. The beauty of the ropes course is that it challenges people to detach from all that is solid and familiar. People become ungrounded, literally, by having to confront safe-but-scary elements suspended forty feet in the air. In addition to requiring a healthy dose of *TRY* Courage, successfully traversing through all the elements requires the full emotional and physical support of your teammates.

Confronting the Pink Elephants in the Room

The adventurous activities of the first day, coupled with a team dinner that evening, helped put everyone's guard down while building up their trust levels. Confronting the Pink Elephants would take *TELL* Courage, and a trustful environment would aid in the process. To set up the conversation on the second day, I first presented the findings of the up-front interviews and then introduced the two Pink Elephants described earlier. To structure the conversation, I set forth a number of rules of engagement, which included *focus on what's best for the company*; *use language to connect, not compete*; *balance honesty with courtesy*; *"go there"*; and *be courageous*. I also let them know that it was my job to broker the conversation, to make certain that people spoke as adults, and to ensure that no one got emotionally body-slammed. Finally, I had each of RadWorks' three principals verbally agree that there would be no repercussions for people telling the truth and that no subject was off-limits.

Once one person says something courageous, it is easier for others to do so. In this instance the first person to step into his *TELL* Courage was Geoff, one of the newer and nervier folks. Geoff had joined RadWorks after graduating with a degree in marketing eighteen months earlier. He spoke of having been attracted to RadWorks' unconventional style and bold approach to innovation. But he had grown disappointed with what he perceived as the senior execs' "selling out" by taking on run-of-the-mill projects that required little marketing thought or rigor. He talked of being frustrated at working long hours on a project that RadWorks had done free for what Geoff called "some lame business development excuse."

Were Geoff's comments stated during a regular office status meeting, RadWorks' principals might have nodded politely and then gone back to their offices and plotted how to get rid of him. But it was clear that underneath Geoff's comments was an appeal for the company to hold itself to higher ideals—ideals upon which the company had been founded.

The Rad in RadWorks stood for *radical*, and Geoff was pointing out that the company was starting to become ordinary. In the marketing world, ordinary is the kiss of death.

Courageous Conversations involve a mature give and take. People acknowledged and validated Geoff's experience. Some voiced counterbalancing perspectives too, pointing out that most companies occasionally have to take on uninspiring projects in the hopes of winning more meaningful work. Lame or not, that's the nature of business development.

Geoff's *TELL* Courage had become an invitation for the group to confront the growing perception that RadWorks was in danger of becoming like the bigger consulting companies it so despised. His candor created a space whereby people became willing to talk about meatier issues. People started "going there"—and the real "there" in this case was the Edict Memo.

Prior to the start of the session, the other NOC MBA faculty and I wondered if the participants would gain enough courage to have a sober and productive conversation about the memo. Of the two Pink Elephants identified before the program, the Edict Memo was the more delicate subject. The memo represented much more than an ill-crafted internal communication. It represented a shift away from the participative leadership style that had characterized RadWorks during its early years to a more "headmaster" leadership approach. Whereas the input of workers had been solicited when facing complex decisions in the past, this time one principal was laying down a company law without any reflection or input from the lower levels—something that would be expected at large, partner-driven consultancies but was entirely unexpected at RadWorks.

"I have something I'd like to say to Doug," began Maria, a talented consultant who had been with the company for three years. Doug, the principal who had written the memo, lifted his eyebrows as if to say, "Me?" Maria continued, "Doug, a lot of people were offended by the memo you sent last month, the one about the new attendance requirements."

Doug was listening but was clearly taken aback. A high achiever, Doug was admired as being much of the reason for RadWorks' success. Because so much of him was personally invested in the business and its reputation, you could see that it was hard for Doug to hear Maria's words. She explained, "A number of us have talked about it, and the thing that bothered us was that it was like a commandment delivered from on high. Like, 'This is how it will be . . . tough shit if you don't like it.' You didn't even invite us to get back to you with questions, which to me meant that you weren't interested in getting any."

This was it. We had arrived at the nexus of courage. The secret was out; the veil had been lifted off the Pink Elephant. What Doug would say next mattered a great deal. Tightening his lips, Doug slowly began, "I'm taken aback. Not angry, but surprised. Maybe a little disappointed too. My recollection is that prior to the memo, during one of our staff meetings, people were expressing concerns about feeling fragmented and disconnected from each other. That bothered me, because as a company we're at a point in time where we need to solidify our identity, our culture. I didn't send the memo based on some power trip. I sent it as a solution for pulling us together."

Truth has depth. The room was heavy and silent. These moments are rare and necessary for groups. It is the kind of silence that no one rushes to fill, a spiritual silence. In such moments, groups are filled with sadness and gratitude at the same time. Sad because by stating what was previously unsaid they have forced a change and pried themselves loose from the past. Grateful because the change that everyone was wanting is now with-

> » Truth has depth that, once told, results in a spiritual silence that can be filled with both sadness and gratitude. »

in reach. Like two people reluctantly admitting that they are in love, from this moment on, for better or worse, RadWorks would be different. Things had gotten serious.

Extending the Value of Courage

After a time, the room became filled with *TELL* Courage. The new people talked about growing tired of hearing about the "good old days" when the company was founded. People voiced a desire to create new stories and new traditions. People started talking about the new culture they wanted to create and started putting definition to the type of work environment they wanted to work within. They started filling up the conference room wall with flip-charted lists of company improvements that they wanted to rally around.

As I told the folks at RadWorks before the program ended, religion is what happens when you leave the church. The NOC MBA experience would have the most impact if people honored the company and themselves by being courageous with each other going forward.

As part of the service, Giant Leap includes a follow-up visit to the client's offices a few weeks after the session. When we met with RadWorks, they told us that they had held three town-hall meetings since the program, all focused on bettering the company and defining its culture. They told us how they were calling this the "summer of thinking," and that everything about the company, from the way communication was handled to the organizational structure, was being reconsidered. Finally, they told us how people had begun using "*TELL* Courage" as a sort of rallying cry to prod people into being more up-front about things instead of letting them fester.

The RadWorks story offers a number of *TELL* Courage bucket-filling applications:

Fill the Other Buckets First: Creating an environment that encourages workers to speak openly and honestly takes time and trust. The people at RadWorks weren't ready to offer *TELL* Courage to one another until they had raised their *trust* levels to a point where the discussion could be safely held. As a manager, work first on getting people to extend themselves (such as with stretch assignments) and building trust (such as delegating meaningful assignments) before expecting them to have *TELL* Courage. *TRY* and *TRUST* are often the means for filling the *TELL* bucket.

Ready Yourself to Be Told: As a manager, you may think you want your workers to have more *TELL* Courage, but when they start telling you things in an unvarnished way, you may find yourself taking it personally. Make a promise to yourself that you will consider each person's words, regardless of how hard they are to hear, without responding rashly or defensively. Have the courage to get told to!

Act on What Is Told: Few things are as frustrating as mustering up the courage to tell your bosses something, only to have it fall on deaf ears. When appropriate and feasible, honor people's *TELL* Courage by taking action on what they say. The principals at RadWorks did this by holding follow-up sessions devoted to hearing about, and taking appropriate actions on, the employees' recommendations.

As described in this chapter, *TELL* Courage is often the hardest to exhibit in a work setting. It is also the hardest bucket for managers to fill. The story about RadWorks shows that getting workers to speak out openly and without reservation is sometimes a function of first filling their *TRY* and *TRUST* buckets.

Next we'll shift our attention away from the specific courage bucket behaviors, and look at ways you can express your courage in all aspects of your personal and professional life. Part 3 of the book focuses on helping you commit to taking more giant leaps in all areas of your life.

Part III

Committing to Giant Leaps

So now you know about courage. Great. But what are you going to do about it? In the book's final section, we shift toward commitment, action, and accountability. We also broaden the reach of your courage capabilities. Chapter 10 focuses on helping you make a commitment to become a Courageous Manager by offering contrasting views of the same work situation. The choice of whether or not to lead others courageously is up to you. This chapter is focused on clarifying your options and introducing you to the consequences, good and bad, that your choice is likely to produce.

Finally, while this book has been largely devoted to courage at work, the book's lessons aren't limited to the workplace. The last chapter, chapter 11, encourages you to adopt a holistic view of courage so that you can integrate the virtue into every area of your life. Chapter 11 also reveals the single most important motivational fact of life, a fact that should drive and inform all of your actions and decisions, and help you to hold yourself accountable for living a courageous life.

Chapter 10

The Courageous Choice

An executive is a person who always decides; sometimes he decides correctly, but he always decides.

John H. Patterson

All of the chapters thus far have led to one fundamental question: Will courage go to work with you or not? *Your answer will have a huge impact on the performance of your people as well as on your own well-being as a manager. The stakes, in short, are high. Thus, before you answer, please consider, by reading these contrasting views, the outcomes that your choice is likely to produce.*

The first version of the story illustrates what the workplace looks and acts like when courage is lacking.

A Tale of Two Teams

Part I: Spilling Buckets

Bzzzzzt.

"Crap. Does this BlackBerry ever sleep? It's 6:30 a.m., for God's sake." You keep one hand on the steering wheel as you reach for your gadget holster. It's your boss.

"Heads up. Tanker is hunting for you. He's PO'd. Nobody on your team submitted their time reports again."

You swallow your last mouthful of latte, thinking to yourself, "Stan Tanker is an ass." Steering the car with your knees, you type, "Thx for the hds up. I'll get on them."

You inch your way through the morning traffic sludge, wondering how things could have gotten this bad. A year ago you couldn't wait to be promoted to manager. Now you feel trapped in your own life. All you hear about are complaints: from your boss, from your customers, and from your employees. This isn't what you signed up for.

By the time you reach the parking lot, you are tight with anxiety. "What the hell is wrong with them?" you think. "No matter how much I get on them about the stupid time reports, they just blow me off. What did I ever do wrong to deserve such a bunch of dregs and losers? No wonder the CFO is pissed off."

A year ago you were full of excitement. The company you work for had just won a huge outsourcing deal. As part of the arrangement, your company would manage the IT function of a large banking client. It seemed like an easy enough proposition. Your company would inherit a thousand employees from the client company and would institute new management rigor to improve operations. Information technology wasn't the bank's core competency, and therefore it wasn't using IT in a way that would create strategic and competitive advantages for the company. The value proposition was that by outsourcing the IT function and by offloading its IT employees to your company, the client would be able to raise output and quality and cut IT costs.

The opportunity had presented you with a chance to fast-track it to manager. All you'd have to do was manage a group of legacy but experienced employees. The challenge would be winning over their hearts and minds so that they could make the transition to full-fledged members of your company's workforce. While people would still be working in their same jobs, alongside their same colleagues, they would no longer work for the bank. It would be critical for you to help them make the cultural shift between the two companies, lest they not make the performance gains that were promised to the client.

The transition turned out to be much harder than you or anyone else expected. First of all, the average age of the outsourced IT employees is forty-six. That wouldn't be much of a problem except that you are thirty-three. Even though they nod politely when you give them direction, you feel like they're secretly thinking, "Who the hell is this chick, telling us how to do jobs that we were doing before she was born?" Second, your company vastly underestimated the cultural challenges. In your company, things move at "eSpeed" and multitasking is a premium skill. But as banking employees, they grew up in a highly regulated environment where all decisions were bumped up to the highest levels before action could be taken. Knowing how to create a paper trail in order to CYA was a critical skill.

As you walk into the building, you sigh, thinking, "Another day at the salt mine. Another day of lame excuses and negative attitudes. Another day of having to micromanage people just so they'll do their jobs. Another day dealing with ungrateful bosses."

"Stan, I'm sorry," you say upon entering his office. "I must have told my group a thousand times to take this time-reporting stuff seriously. It's just that time reporting is a new concept to them. The bank didn't use a time-tracking system. All of us managers are finding it hard getting them to comply with our policies. They just won't try new things." Stan winces, as though he's smelling bad cheese. "I've heard that they think we're tracking their time because we don't trust them. But no one asks any questions when I tell them why we're doing it, so . . . "

Dismissively, Stan rolls his hand in little circles, trying to get you to fast-forward to the point. "If I had a meat cleaver, I'd slice that hand right off your puny little body," you say in your head. Out loud you say, "Sorry, Stan. I'll get on them."

"Once again," you think, "instead of telling Stan what a jerk he is, I bite my tongue. Who the hell does that twerp think he is, putting me on fast forward? And what's wrong with me that I let myself get so afraid of him?"

When you get to your workstation, everyone is oblivious to the crow you just ate. "Hey," you say, at a volume high enough to get people's attention. "Do you realize the shovelful of crap I just got from Stan Tanker about your late time reports? What are you, a bunch of grown-up kindergartners? How many times do I have to tell you to turn in your frickin' time reports? Do you realize that our company bills the bank based on the data in those reports? When you don't do them, we can't bill them. Here's the new rule: Submit your time reports on time or I'll fire you. Does anyone have a problem with that?"

No one says a word.

This second version of the story shows what happens when courage permeates throughout the workforce. Hopefully you'll find it more reflective of the environment you work in.

A Tale of Two Teams

Part II: Full-Bucket Management

Bzzzzzt.

"Crap. Does this BlackBerry ever sleep? It's 6:30 a.m., for God's sake." You keep one hand on the steering wheel as you reach for your gadget holster. It's Stan Tanker.

"Come to my office when you get in."

Steering the car with your knees, you type, "Will do."

As you inch your way through the morning traffic sludge, you think back to a year ago, when you would have misinterpreted Stan's short message as terse or disrespectful. But over the last year, and since "the talk," you've come to appreciate Stan's no-nonsense style. "Stan doesn't contact me directly much," you think, "so it must be important."

When you think back to "the talk," it's almost as though you had been standing outside your body watching yourself when it happened. Just under a year ago, Stan had walked into your work area while you were on the phone with a key client, but instead of waiting for you to finish the call, he abruptly said, "Get off the phone; I need to talk to you." Though you politely apologized to your client about having to get back to him, you knew that this was your chance to set a boundary with Stan. A mentor had suggested that you'd never amount to much of a manager if you didn't have the courage to assert yourself to your bosses. "In the long run," your mentor had told you, "ass kissing is career killing."

Looking back with the hindsight of a year, it seems surreal, as if some braver you had taken over your body. You stood ten inches from Stan, looked him intently in the eyes, and said, "Stan, we need to talk. But not here. Let's go to a small conference room." Stan visibly shook his head, like you had just tapped his jaw with a little punch. But, surprisingly, he followed you.

"Listen, Stan," you began, "I know you're going to tell me something important; I respect that. But before you do, I need to say something to you. It is not okay to interrupt me— in fact, it's completely disrespectful and unprofessional. From now on, if you need to get my attention when I'm talking to someone else, just give me a quick heads-up. I promise I'll make it a priority to get back to you."

It seemed like time had slowed to a stop before Stan answered you. He tilted his head, squinted slightly, and then, after exhaling, said, "I know, I know. Things are moving way too fast and I'm under the gun. I know I come on strong sometimes; it's not you. There are just a lot of loose items that I can't afford to drop right now."

In his own way, Stan had given you an apology. From that moment on, things were different between you and Stan. So now, a year later, you actually feel eager to find out what he wants to talk about.

By the time you reach the parking lot, you are ready for the day. "This managing stuff is actually fun," you think. "I mean, how many people get to interact directly with the CFO? How cool is that? And how many people get to lead a team of such experienced professionals? My team blows me away!"

As you walk into the building, you smile a bit, thinking back to the early days of the project. Though things got off to a rocky start, you learned a lot in the past year. You learned, for example, that the best way to get people to try new things is to give them a voice in shaping how those things will be done. The time reports were a good example. One of the reasons why people resisted the idea was that it wasn't always clear how to allocate their time. Each activity was supposed to match a specific job code, but a lot of time-consuming tasks, like generating management reports or attending company outings, didn't have job codes. So employees were basically forced to lie about where they spent the time for tasks that lacked job codes. But after you recognized that forcing employees to comply with a flawed system was unfair to them, and after you started praising them whenever they took the initiative to create solutions to inefficiencies that they identified, they became more proactive in their approach. For example, the team came up with a list of suggested job codes for the unaccounted-for tasks, which you then presented to Stan. In the process, not only did your team make a positive impression on the CFO, but the changes they had suggested made a positive impact on the entire IT organization as well.

You also learned that people trust you more when you put your ego aside. Turns out your micromanaging style had as much to do with your pride as it did with your need to control things. The truest reason for grabbing tasks back was that you were afraid the mistakes of other people would impact how you were judged as a manager. You had a reputation to protect! But in the process of protecting your ego, your behavior sent a strong message to your employees that you didn't trust them. Had it not been for all the comments you had gotten on a confidential 360-degree leadership feedback survey, you might never have learned the importance of letting go and trusting your team.

Reflecting back, the biggest lesson you learned during the past year was that your job is to manage how people respond to comfort and fear, and that the best way to do that is to focus on building their courage. As you have attempted to be more courageous yourself, your team's courage has grown, too. With courage, your team members look forward to new challenges. With courage, team members trust that each other's intentions are positive. With courage, people talk to each other respectfully but assertively. Courage has become, for you and the team, a positive energizer. So by the time you reach Stan's office, you're ready for whatever challenge he throws your way.

"Hey Stan, what's up?" you say after entering his office.

"Oh, hi. Come on in. Listen, our banking client called me this morning, and you're not going to believe this, but it seems that the improved performance of our IT department has caught their attention." Stan is grinning like a kid on the verge of revealing a secret.

"And . . . ?" you playfully say.

"And, they want our IT department to help them implement a time-reporting system in their company!" Stan smiles, tickled by the irony. "So, given your team's hard-earned experiences with time reporting last year, I figured it would be the best one to lead the project. The bank wants us to start by creating an FAQ document and hosting a series of learning forums to help their employees prepare for the changes."

"That's amazing, Stan. You know my team will be up for it. But before I go back to them, there's one question that I need to ask you because I know they'll ask me—"

"Yes!" he interrupts, and then smiles sheepishly. "Um, sorry. I just knew what you were going to ask. Yes, I've already created a job code for this work."

Courageous managers are sorely needed in the workplace. But becoming one means making a choice, and then committing yourself to living courageously, despite the constant pressures that comfort and fear present. What will your choice be?

Now What?

Well, here we are. You, hopefully, contemplating all you've read and standing at the threshold of a choice. Me hoping that I can help you with the most important career high dive you'll ever take.

After you've considered the contrasting stories above, I hope the merits of courageous management are obvious. When your behaviors are directed by courageous impulses, you are operating out of your best and braver self. When other people witness your newfound behaviors and the positive results the behaviors cause, they gradually step into their own courage, too. As they do, the energy level of your team lifts. People begin engaging with one another with honesty, accuracy, and passion. A can-do spirit takes hold as people start to support one another. "Problems" are increasingly viewed as opportunities and challenges. Workers begin to initiate forward-moving projects to advance the goals of the team, department, and organization. The work environment becomes imbued with a feeling of momentum. Courage refreshes, recharges, and recommits workers to their projects, teammates, and careers.

In light of such benefits, the decision to pursue management by courage would seem obvious. But we both know that opting for courage means holding yourself to higher standards and ideals, which comes with its own set of challenges and realities. As you grapple with your decision of whether to become a courageous manager, here are some additional considerations to help you make an informed choice:

- **Be Careful What You Wish For:** The CEO of an insurance company once asked me to work with one of his VPs in hopes of helping the VP to become more assertive. He was considering the VP as a possible successor but was worried that the VP didn't have enough executive presence and that he wasn't tough enough. Before agreeing to coach the VP, I told the CEO that when the VP became more assertive, it might not come in the exact form that the CEO expected. I explained that early on, the CEO himself might become the target of the VP's assertiveness, which he might find unsettling. The CEO claimed he understood.

    Sure enough, after about two months of coaching the VP, I got a call from the CEO. "Bill," he said, "I'm troubled by a rather acerbic e-mail that I got from Rodney yesterday. He basically told me that I am perceived as coming off as disrespectful when dealing with the people in his division. Frankly, I was offended. He works for me, not the other way around."

I reminded the CEO about the conversation we'd had before the coaching process began. Rodney was just doing what the CEO had asked for—being more assertive and tough . . . only tough on the CEO. For the CEO it was a big lesson in how easy it is to want to put people back in the same box that we found them in, even after encouraging them to escape from the box.

This whole book has been dedicated to helping you build your people's courage. Well, guess what? They'll probably start being more courageous! As they spread their courage wings, the changes you get will defy the preexisting definition you already have of them—for better or for worse. When employees are more courageous, they won't sit in their cubicles taking orders like well-trained circus animals. Their courage won't always be directed in ways you can control. Courageous employees will press to take on more challenging roles. Courageous employees will voice their opinions and objections more freely. Courageous employees will challenge, and aspire, and risk, and think, and *lead*. While that may look inviting on the surface, it could also make them hold *you* to a higher standard.

- **You'll Need More Than Courage:** If all you want to be is courageous, go stick a sword down your throat. Courage without brains is like ethics without a soul. There's smart courage and there's stupid courage. Just because you're courageous doesn't mean you're applying your courage toward the right aims or in the right way. Undisciplined courage is a wild beast.

You'll notice that I haven't spent much time talking about morality in this book. The way I see it, *you* have to bring the morality to the courage. And you should. If the early 2000s taught us anything, it is that the immorality of a handful of senior-level individuals can corrupt entire organizations and institutions. Courage, like power, leadership, and ambition, can be a misused means to an immoral end.

Courage takes its fullest and noblest form when it is shaped and tempered by intelligence, discipline, focus, and morality. As a manager, you would be wise to build these things in your people, too.

- **Get Ready to Enter Naysayer Territory:** Just as often as courage wins admiration, it provokes anger and outrage. Certainly the people who marched in Selma, Alabama, were being courageous. But they were also spit at, sprayed with water hoses, attacked with dogs, and beaten with clubs . . . in many instances by the very people who were supposed to protect them: law enforcement. The courage that brings out the best in you or your employees may bring out the worst in others.

  Naysayers surround courageous people the way zombies surround the hero in a horror movie. For example, I coached the medical director of a hospital who oversaw a staff of a hundred but who hated his job of twenty years. His secret desire was to become a high school teacher. What stood in his way? His naysaying wife. She'd harp on him, complaining, "You want to give up your six-figure salary to become a poorly paid teacher? Forget it!"

Naysayers often position their opposition as being in your best interest. "But you might get hurt! I'm only trying to protect you!" they say. More often than not, though, they are trying to protect themselves. Their real worry is that *your* courage will cause *them* harm. The deepest concern of the medical director's wife, for example, wasn't her husband's well-being; it was losing a lifestyle to which she had become accustomed.

Having said that, let's recognize that for every ten naysayers there will be at least one powerful *yeasayer* cheering from the sidelines. So powerful, in fact, that his or her cheering will likely have a counterbalancing, and possibly neutralizing, effect on all those naysayers. Courage is inspirational and attractive. Courage inspires because, like leadership, it is an *aspirational* concept. We all have a certain unused capacity to be even more courageous. So when we see others using their capacity to the fullest, we feel a mixture of awe and envy. By being courageous, they are confronting the very fears that are still gripping us. Thus we have a vested interest in their success; their courage just might provide us with the solution to our fears.

- **A Moment of Courage Can Have an Enduring Career Impact:** I once asked a senior executive whom I was coaching about the most courageous thing he had ever done at work. He replied, "That would have to be when I came out of the closet.

"Let me tell you something, it was a different world twenty years ago," he explained. "I wasn't about to wave my rainbow flag and bring attention to myself. So for years I went on pretending I was someone who I wasn't. And I hated it. The more time went on, the guiltier I felt for betraying myself. Eventually I realized that no job is important enough for me to have to come to work as a fraud each day."

For the executive, one singular courageous moment would impact the rest of his life. Had he continued shying away from that moment, he would have moved from self-betrayal to self-contempt. To live a fulfilling life, one has to be able to live within his or her own skin. By coming out, the executive was being respectful to himself. He was saying, "I am not willing to hide who I am just to make you comfortable. This is who I am, and I am not going to pretend to be someone I am not." The temporary anguish he went through as he walked into his courage (in this case, *TRUST* Courage, because he was trusting himself) has been eclipsed by an enduring sense of satisfaction that comes from knowing that he stood up for himself.

One moment of courage can change the entire trajectory of your life. This courage stuff is serious business! When you decide to start your own business, or buck for a promotion, or quit your six-figure job to become a teacher, you're going to be a very different person in the long run.

So, are you inching toward the edge of your decision? Are you ready to join the Fraternal Order of Courageous

Managers? I sure hope so. Here's why: *The world of work needs more courageous executives.* It's true. Here we are in the twenty-first century, with unprecedented access to leading-edge management knowledge—knowledge that has been accumulating, maturing, and assumedly evolving for hundreds of years—and yet too many people in too many organizations are profoundly unhappy. Despite advancements in nearly every aspect of organizational life, for all its progressiveness the modern organization remains hopelessly backward when it comes to the treatment of people. It makes no difference whether you work for an aging institution or a groovy start-up venture with a foosball table in the middle of the office; when pressures mount and dollars dwindle, too many managers succumb to controlling and abusive behavior as the primary means of motivating workers. Such behavior takes neither courage nor intelligence. In fact, it takes the abdication of those things, giving in to base impulses.

You and your courage are needed because *you* have the best chance of bringing positive change to the world of work. The fact is, whether you respect them or not, your bosses will eventually retire from the workforce. When they do, *you* will move into their place. What will you do with all that power and responsibility? How will you do things differently than your bosses did? What kind of role model will you be? What will your employees learn from you by the way you treat them? What kinds of changes will you advocate and promote? What will you stand for and against? When you get ready to leave the workforce, what impact will you hope to have had? How might having more courage impact how you answer all those questions?

The Courageous Commitment

If your aspiration is to progress to higher levels in your organization, if you aim to have a greater and more positive impact on those around you, and if you are ready to respond to comfort and fear with greater backbone, then now is the time to sign the following declaration:

From this moment forward, I will deliberately take on work challenges that put me outside my comfort zone. I will place greater trust in the people I lead, and in the people who lead me. I will speak more freely and assertively, even when doing so may be unpopular with others.

From this moment forward, I will search for opportunities to fill the courage buckets of each worker I am responsible for. I will provide meaningful work challenges that stretch their capabilities so that they can demonstrate TRY *Courage. I will be candid and consistent and deliver on my promises so that people can have more* TRUST *Courage. I will create an environment of* TELL *Courage, where people can express themselves honestly and assertively, regardless of whether their opinions are aligned with my own.*

From this moment forward, I will be a Courageous Manager.

Signed: _____

Today's Date: _____

Date When You Will Evaluate Your Progress: _____

Chapter 11

Courageous Living

I shall not fear anyone on Earth.

Mahatma Gandhi, nonviolent revolutionary

Be Courageous!

Bill Treasurer, high-diving, Speedo-wearing,
fear-carrying courage consultant

"You have cancer."

Few words fill the brain with as much unsettling confusion as *cancer*. Pretty much everything my doctor said after that was a jumble. "Positive biopsy . . . tumors . . . unusual for your age . . . radical surgery . . ."

One comment did get through, however: "If you don't treat this, you will die."

There are advantages to running a courage-building company. Courage is an attractive subject, and it certainly has attracted some marquee clients to Giant Leap. Conversations become electrified when they turn to the subject of courage. It is a subject that pulls people forward and upward, elevating them to higher ideals and standards. But there are disadvantages to running a courage-building company, too. Courage is a subject with considerable mass and gravity. My proximity to the subject seems to have attracted an unusually large number of challenging life experiences. I sometimes wonder if, when God found out I was going to devote my life to helping others to be more courageous, he thought, "Is that so? Then I guess Mr. Treasurer is going to need some lessons in that area. Angels, start the conveyor belt!"

Not that God causes cancer. That was likely traceable to my male ancestors. Most men who get prostate cancer, the deadliest cancer among men after lung cancer, don't have to look too far up the ladder of their male lineage to find another cancer heir.

When I started writing this book, I had no idea that the subject of courage would hit me in such a personal way. But I guess I should have expected it. When I wrote *Right Risk*, I was grappling with the decision of whether to leave Accenture to start my own company. Writing the book helped me to work myself through the risk. Fortunately, according to the many correspondences I received after the book was published, the book helped many others to take purposeful risks, too.

But leaving a company is one thing; having cancer at forty-five years old is another. It brings a new dimension to the idea of courage that I hadn't considered—namely, the importance of persisting through suffering. The hard part about having cancer is living with a giant scythe-shaped question mark hanging over your head. This isn't some momentary or episodic act of courage. This is courage stretched and extended over a vast sea of unknowingness. Even for cancer "survivors"—a designation you receive only after five consecutive years without a cancer reoccurrence—there is no definitive sense of resolution. The hungry bastard can always come back. Nope, this is a kind of courage you have to settle in with for the long haul.

The Most Important Motivational Fact

I was thrilled when Sara Blakely offered to write the foreword to this book. Sara is a kindred spirit and an amazing person. She breaks every stereotype you could have about a person who founded an international retail enterprise. She is kind-hearted, unassuming, down-to-earth, and generous. She is also courageous. As she noted in the foreword, part of her courage stems from her refusal to let fear hold her back. She gets afraid as much as everyone else (she would say more), but she presses forward despite her fears.

Sara and I had a long talk once about the sources of courage and why some people seem more willing to accept the challenges that courage inevitably brings. We agreed that the answer is the most motivational fact of all, which I'll share with you in a moment. It has to do with life's fragile and fleeting nature.

It turns out that one of the reasons for Sara's willingness to respond to life and business with courage is that she had, in her own words, a "shift in consciousness" as a result of a horrible tragedy that occurred when she was sixteen. As she was crossing the street with one of her best friends, a car veered out of control and smashed into the girl, killing her instantly. Sara's mind reeled with shock as she tried to comprehend the enormity of what had just happened.

Sara describes the tragedy as her personal 9/11. One moment she was laughing with her lively friend; the next she was watching her die. In a visceral way, the tragic event taught Sara how fragile, chancy, and potentially brief life is.

Tragedy, if you let it, can offer you life-seasoning lessons. Over time, Sara has come to believe that an acute awareness of your own mortality can be a liberating thing. The knowledge that life can end instantly—and at a time over which you have absolutely no control—provides reason enough to live courageously. When you know that your tomorrows are not guaranteed, you stop using "I'll do it tomorrow" as an excuse to postpone your dreams.

So what is the most motivational fact of all? You guessed it: *You are going to die someday!*

Living a Life You Can Be Proud to Call Your Own

In 2008, a movie called *The Bucket List* was released, starring Jack Nicholson and Morgan Freeman. The two play terminally ill cancer patients who escape from a hospital, setting out to accomplish a list of adventurous things before they kick the bucket. The movie's premise connects directly to courage. When you become keenly aware of life's brevity, you become more willing to live it courageously.

This idea, that the knowledge of your mortality can inspire courageous behavior, was also captured in Tim McGraw's chart-topping country song "Live Like You Were Dying." The song tells the story of a man who, after learning he has cancer, starts living in a courageous way. He goes skydiving, mountain climbing, and even bull riding. But he also loves with more depth and forgives with more generosity. What makes the song so powerful is that it is based on McGraw's own life experiences. The country singer is the son of New York Mets baseball legend Tug McGraw. The song was written just after the elder McGraw died of brain cancer. The singer had taken care of his father during his illness.

So what does all this talk about death and cancer have to do with living courageously? Everything. You and I know that if you knew you had only one more year to live, you would respond to the world very differently than you do today. And that response would be entirely courageous. I'm sure you'd try more things, like traveling to exotic places or learning how to ride a motorcycle. I'm sure you'd make amends to people and open yourself up to trusting them more fully. I'm sure you'd express yourself with less care as to what people think of your opinions. In short, you would behave with more *TRY*, *TRUST*, and *TELL* courage.

Now, dear reader, I recognize that the death-awareness lesson can be carried only so far. This book has focused mostly on applying courage in a work setting. If you really did have only a year to live, you'd probably quit your job and move to Tahiti. The point I'm trying to make is that personally and professionally it is important to live a life, and craft a career, that you can be proud to call your own, because someday both will be gone forever. The life-orienting and potentially courage-inducing fact that you're going to die someday has to do with accountability. Doing things you can be proud of, saying things you can be proud of, and touching the hearts of others in a way you can be proud of are ultimately ways of demonstrating personal and career accountability. At work and at home, doing courageous things is the best way to honor the life you've been blessed with.

All of this relates to how you manage people, too. Your employees are entitled to have a fulfilling career. That's right, *entitled*! They bear much of the responsibility for crafting a fulfilling career. But you, as a manager, also bear some responsibility. Helping them to be courageous in the service of the company's goals is not enough. You have to help them to be courageous in the service of *their* career goals, too. As a manager, you can do both by holding them accountable to their own potential, and providing them with meaningful and courage-inducing challenges. You have to fill them with courage.

Be Courageous!

I want you to live a long, healthy, and courageous life. And I want you to have a long, prosperous, and courageous career. I really do. What I don't want is for you to have career and life longevity only to end up sitting on a barstool someday, complaining about all the things you wish you had done. Regrets, especially over things we *should* have done but didn't because we were too comfortable or afraid when we faced them, burn hot in our souls. The risks we regret the most are always the ones we didn't take.

The motto of Giant Leap Consulting is *Be Courageous!* In my opinion, no two words are more important to life and work. I encourage people to think of those two words when facing challenging situations, intimidating people, or moments of hardship. *Be Courageous!* when you want to ask for a raise. *Be Courageous!* when you need to deliver a tough message to an errant employee. *Be Courageous!* when you suffer a career setback. *Be Courageous!* when you are thinking about transferring overseas. *Be Courageous!* when situations or people try to compromise your integrity. *Be Courageous!* when you or someone else is being bullied. *Be Courageous!* when you are deciding whether to start your own business. In work and in life, for yourself and for others, in all you do and say, *Be Courageous!*

The good news is, you've already had a lot of courageous life experiences to draw from. In other words, *you already are courageous!* Courage has been living inside you since the day you were born. You were courageous on your first day of school. You were courageous when you learned how to drive a car. You were courageous when you first kissed someone, and later when you lost your virginity! You were courageous when you left home for college. You were courageous when you said "I do," and later when you bought a home. You were courageous when you went on your first job interview, became a manager, and led a huge project for your company. You were courageous every time you were afraid and uncomfortable but carried on anyway. All you have to do now is more of what your whole life has been teaching you to do: *Be Courageous!*

As I mentioned in the last chapter, the workplace needs your courage. But the rest of your world needs it, too. Courage goes to work wherever you take it. Whether at home, in your place of worship, on the racquetball court, in your civic organizations, or in your community, your courage is always needed. Think what the world would look like with less fear and more courage.

Fill Up Your World

So where do you start? Start where you are. Start today. Start now. Start by taking a long, hard look at your life and asking yourself, "Where am I playing it too safe? What areas of my life have become annoyingly comfortable? Which of my fears are outdated or inflated? What kind of experiences am I filling my life with? What actions can I take, will I take, am I taking, to be courageous?"

Start by filling *yourself* up with courage. Jump First. Do one thing each day that challenges you, discomforts you, or frightens you. Seek out experiences, big and small, that make your palms sweat. Try some, trust some, tell some, fail some. Invite others to join you. Courage works if you work it. So work it.

Coeur, Corazón, Courage = HEART

As of the writing of this book, I can't tell you whether I will survive cancer. I can tell you that a few months ago I underwent a radical prostatectomy and had my prostate surgically removed. I can also tell you, thankfully, that the prognosis is good. Still, it will be nearly five years before I can officially be called a cancer "survivor."

There is something else I can tell you. Cancer is teaching me an important lesson about how being courageous when facing adversity is made much, much easier with the encouragement of those who care about you. I have been profoundly humbled by the outpouring of support I've received from friends, loved ones, and clients. They have become my community of encouragement and filled me with courage. Plus,

I've got a lot to live for—like the giggles of my three beautiful children, the tender embraces of my loving wife, fantastic and interesting friends, and an incredibly gratifying career. Who knows, maybe cancer will enlarge my understanding of courage. Maybe my cancer experience will help me to better serve my mission of helping people and organizations to *Be More Courageous.*

The question of whether I'll survive cancer is really beside the point. I'm just trying to live a life that brings me smiles and a faster heartbeat—a courageous life. That goal, and the courage that informs it, was what caused me to become a high diver, write a book about risk taking and now another on courage, take up kayaking, quit drinking fifteen years ago, make amends with people I had hurt, launch a business, and move to Asheville, North Carolina. Life is about living. The dying part is just a loud stopwatch ticking in the background.

Your stopwatch is ticking, too. So get on with living . . . courageously!

Acknowledgments

People assign too much credit when they refer to the founder of a company as being courageous. The real person of courage is the person who joins second, when the company is still an infant. I am grateful that Ahli Moore, now Giant Leap Consulting's president, comes to work each day with the same courage he did when he leapt into Giant Leap's business.

The team of professionals at Giant Leap Consulting deserves thanks for helping to bring our mission to life, and for the fun and intelligence you bring the business. This includes the good folks at the Nantahala Outdoor Center (NOC), our partners in delivering Giant Leap's Management By Adventure program.

If the size of a person's challenge is a measure of his courage, then Steve Piersanti, my publisher, is a superhero. The mission of Berrett-Koehler Publishers is "creating a world that works for all." Steve may look like Clark Kent, but he leaps over obstacles like a caped crusader. Thank you, Steve, for holding me accountable to higher standards. Thanks, too, to the wonderful team at Berrett-Koehler, including the review team, who used much *TELL* Courage in giving me feedback about the book. Your hard work makes it easy to be an author.

A special thanks goes out to Mark Levy, founder of Levy Innovation, a marketing strategy company. My work as a courage-building consultant wouldn't have been possible without

Mark's keen insights and bold, precise, and thought-provoking questions. Mark's *TELL* Courage bucket spilleth over!

I am grateful for Giant Leap's courageous clients. I am honored that you have brought us into your worlds and allowed us to know your hopes, fears, and secrets. We are grateful for all of our clients, but especially grateful for those people who go out of their way to help us be successful in their organizations—namely, Charles Lang, Mike Calihan, Steve Rivi, Lynn Morgan, Tina Meyer, Sandra Alexander, Craig Atkinson, Mike Neusch, Duane Hemmerle, and Bob Schacht.

Few things build up people's courage as much as the communities that surround them. I am grateful for my kayaking and high-diving buddies, the Berrett-Koehler Authors Cooperative, and my classmates in Leadership Asheville 26. With friends like you, who could be afraid?

A special thanks goes out to Dr. David Albala of Duke University Hospital, for his robotic wizardry and for helping me to put heaven on hold.

A debt of gratitude goes to Bruce Cockburn for his luscious instrumental soundtrack *Speechless*. Writing this book was much easier when listening to fast-fingered masterpieces like "Train in the Rain." I am also grateful to Hal White, my big-hearted compadre, for turning me on to Bruce Cockburn, RatDog, kayaking, the NOC, and Asheville.

I am most grateful for the people who bring my life meaning, refuge, and joy: my wife, Shannon, and our three spirited children, Alex, Bina, and Ian. My sisters, Karen and Jeannie, and my brother, Doug, also deserve thanks for their lifelong love and support. Finally, my parents, Toby and Bill, deserve special thanks for helping me to navigate through life's rough seas, such as those in the Tropic of Cancer.

Index

About the Author

Bill Treasurer is the founder and chief encouragement officer of Giant Leap Consulting, Inc., a courage-building company. Bill is the author of *Right Risk: 10 Powerful Principles for Taking Giant Leaps with Your Life* (Berrett-Koehler Publishers, 2003), a book about personal courage. He is also the chief editor of *Positively M.A.D.: Making a Difference in Your Organizations, Communities, and the World* (Berrett-Koehler Publishers, 2004), a compilation of stories from world-renowned experts that inspire readers to make a positive difference in their organizations.

Bill's insights have been featured in more than one hundred newspapers, including the *Washington Post*, the *New York Daily News*, the *Chicago Tribune*, the *Atlanta Journal Constitution*, the *Boston Herald*, and *Investor's Business Daily*. Bill's ideas have also appeared in such magazines as *Woman's Day*, *Business to Business*, *Redbook*, *Fitness*, and *Harvard Management Update*.

Since 1991, Bill has been strengthening people's leadership skills, improving team performance, and helping executives to behave more courageously. Among others, Bill has facilitated sessions for CNN, Starbucks, GE, Chrysler, Toyota, Bank of America, the Home Depot, Credit Suisse First Boston, the U.S. Drug Enforcement Administration (DEA), and the U.S. Department of Veterans Affairs.

Prior to founding Giant Leap, Bill was an executive in Accenture's change-management and human-performance practice, eventually becoming the company's first internal executive coach. He began his career as a leadership consultant with High Performing Systems, Inc., and as a team-building instructor with Executive Adventure, Inc.

Before getting a "real job," Bill traveled the world as a member of the U.S. High Diving Team. During that time, he performed more than fifteen hundred high dives, from heights that topped one hundred feet. More than three hundred dives were performed while on fire (see the cover of *Right Risk* as proof)!

Bill holds a master's degree in administrative science from the University of Wisconsin at Green Bay and an undergraduate degree from West Virginia University, where he attended school on a full athletic scholarship for springboard diving.

Bill lives in Asheville, North Carolina, with his wife, Shannon, and their three children, Alex, Bina, and Ian. When he isn't working with clients, he enjoys jumping on the trampoline with his kids and going whitewater kayaking on the beautiful rivers of western North Carolina.

To inquire about having Bill speak about courage as it relates to your organization, contact btreasurer@giantleapconsulting.com.

About Giant Leap Consulting

Giant Leap Consulting (GLC), Inc., is a courage-building company whose mission is to help people and organizations to *Be More Courageous*. GLC leads strategic planning efforts, designs and develops leadership programs, facilitates team-building workshops, and delivers customized training workshops. Founded in 2002, GLC has amassed a client list that includes, among others, Accenture, EarthLink, Manheim, SPANX, American Family Insurance, Merial, the Centers for Disease Control, Equity Office Properties, Aldridge Electric Inc., ComEd, Walsh Construction, Meade, Spirit Airlines, IBM, UNICEF, and the U.S. Department of Veterans Affairs.

To inquire about having Giant Leap Consulting build courage in your organization, contact info@giantleapconsulting.com or call 800-867-7239.

Visit the *Courage Goes to Work* Web Site

To learn more about how to apply the concepts from this book, visit www.couragegoestowork.com. As a reader of this book, you are entitled to download additional material, including a list of expert tips on how to be more courageous and a guide to more effective risk taking. You will also have access to a free webinar that elaborates on many of the book's ideas. To use this material, click on the "Members Login" tab and use the following password: *courage*.

Other books by Bill Treasurer

Right Risk

Ten powerful principles for taking Giant Leaps with your life.

Positively M.A.D.

Making a difference in your organizations, communities, and the world. Stories and ideas from 50 of today's leading experts, and edited by Bill Treasurer.

About Berrett-Koehler Publishers

Berrett-Koehler is an independent publisher dedicated to an ambitious mission: Creating a World That Works for All.

We believe that to truly create a better world, action is needed at all levels—individual, organizational, and societal. At the individual level, our publications help people align their lives with their values and with their aspirations for a better world. At the organizational level, our publications promote progressive leadership and management practices, socially responsible approaches to business, and humane and effective organizations. At the societal level, our publications advance social and economic justice, shared prosperity, sustainability, and new solutions to national and global issues.

A major theme of our publications is "Opening Up New Space." They challenge conventional thinking, introduce new ideas, and foster positive change. Their common quest is changing the underlying beliefs, mindsets, institutions, and structures that keep generating the same cycles of problems, no matter who our leaders are or what improvement programs we adopt.

We strive to practice what we preach—to operate our publishing company in line with the ideas in our books. At the core of our approach is *stewardship*, which we define as a deep sense of responsibility to administer the company for the benefit of all of our "stakeholder" groups: authors, customers, employees, investors, service providers, and the communities and environment around us.

We are grateful to the thousands of readers, authors, and other friends of the company who consider themselves to be part of the "BK Community." We hope that you, too, will join us in our mission.

Be Connected

Visit Our Website

Go to www.bkconnection.com to read exclusive previews and excerpts of new books, find detailed information on all Berrett-Koehler titles and authors, browse subject-area libraries of books, and get special discounts.

Subscribe to Our Free E-Newsletter

Be the first to hear about new publications, special discount offers, exclusive articles, news about bestsellers, and more! Get on the list for our free e-newsletter by going to www.bkconnection.com.

Get Quantity Discounts

Berrett-Koehler books are available at quantity discounts for orders of ten or more copies. Please call us toll-free at (800) 929-2929 or e-mail us at bkp.orders@aidcvt.com.

Host a Reading Group

For tips on how to form and carry on a book reading group in your workplace or community, see our website at www.bkconnection.com.

Join the BK Community

Thousands of readers of our books have become part of the "BK Community" by participating in events featuring our authors, reviewing draft manuscripts of forthcoming books, spreading the word about their favorite books, and supporting our publishing program in other ways. If you would like to join the BK Community, please contact us at bkcommunity@bkpub.com.